The Story of the

in France

Enos Herbert Glynne Roberts

Alpha Editions

This edition published in 2024

ISBN : 9789362997548

Design and Setting By
Alpha Editions
www.alphaedis.com
Email - info@alphaedis.com

As per information held with us this book is in Public Domain.
This book is a reproduction of an important historical work. Alpha Editions uses the best technology to reproduce historical work in the same manner it was first published to preserve its original nature. Any marks or number seen are left intentionally to preserve its true form.

Contents

CHAPTER I. England. ....- 1 -

CHAPTER II. The 1st Division. ....- 6 -

CHAPTER III. The 55th Division. ....- 19 -

CHAPTER IV. The 57th Division. ....- 57 -

APPENDIX. ....- 76 -

CHAPTER I.
ENGLAND.

Shortly after the commencement of the Volunteer Movement in 1859, many members of the newspaper and printing trades in Liverpool were desirous of forming a regiment composed of men connected with those businesses. A meeting was held in the Liverpool Town Hall, and the scheme was so well received that steps were taken towards the formation of a corps. Sanction was obtained, and on the 21st February, 1861, the officers and men of the new unit took the oath of allegiance at St. George's Hall. Thus came into being the 80th Lancashire Rifle Volunteers, and on the 2nd April, 1863, the 73rd Battalion of the Lancashire Rifle Volunteers was amalgamated with it. In the early days of its existence the new unit attended reviews and inspections at Mount Vernon, Newton-le-Willows and Aintree. Some time afterwards it was renumbered the 19th Lancashire Rifle Volunteers. Later—in 1888—it became the 6th Volunteer Battalion of The King's (Liverpool Regiment).

The early parades of the Regiment took place at Rose Hill Police Station, and the Corn Exchange, Brunswick Street, until Headquarters were established at 16, Soho Street.

To those who took part in these parades great credit and thanks are due. Through their efforts an organised battalion came into being, men were trained for the bearing of arms and the defence of their country should the occasion ever arise, and the soldierly spirit was inculcated in many who followed a civilian occupation. Those who survived until the Great War, though not privileged to lead on the battlefield, had at any rate the satisfaction of realising that their work was not in vain. Directly attributable to the efforts of the early volunteers is the fact that in 1915 the Territorial Force was ready for the reinforcement of the Regular Army in the Western Theatre of the War, and this afforded the New Armies which Lord Kitchener had formed ample time for the completion of their training.

In 1884 the Headquarters in Soho Street were changed for more commodious and better equipped premises at 59, Everton Road, where the Battalion remained domiciled until 1914. During the South African War the Battalion sent out a company, and the experience the men gained there proved very useful at the annual camps. Several of the men who went to South Africa were privileged to serve in the next war. On the formation of the Territorial Force the Battalion was once again renumbered and henceforth it was known as the 9th Battalion of The King's (Liverpool Regiment) Territorial Force.

The recruiting area of the Battalion embraced the Everton district of Liverpool, a locality inhabited chiefly by members of the tradesmen and artisan classes, which furnished the Regiment with the bulk of its recruits. There was a detachment located in the country at Ormskirk, from which the Battalion drew some of its finest fighting material. Agriculturalists make good soldiers, and this was evidenced on many occasions later by the behaviour and ability of the men from this town. In the ranks there was a sprinkling of sailors and miners, whose several callings equipped them with knowledge which proved useful in their new profession. The officers for the most part were drawn from the professional class and business houses of the city.

There came on the 4th August, 1914, a telegram to Headquarters containing only the one word "Mobilize." On that day Great Britain declared war on Germany. Notices were sent out ordering the men to report, and at 2-0 p.m. on the 6th there was only one man unaccounted for. The mobilization was satisfactory.

Difficulties immediately presented themselves, for the men had to be housed and fed. The first night the men spent in the Hippodrome Theatre, where the artists gave them a special performance in addition to the public performances. Afterwards sleeping accommodation was found in the Liverpool College. Through the kindness of the committee of the Newsboys' Home in Everton Road arrangements were made to feed the men. There were too many for them to be fed all at once, so that meals had to be taken in relays. At Headquarters there was a certain amount of congestion, for equipment, picks, shovels and other mobilization stores took up a considerable amount of room. Besides this there were collected at Headquarters civilian milk floats, lorries, spring carts and other vehicles which had been pressed into service as regimental transport. Horses with patched civilian harness gave the transport the appearance of a "haywire outfit." After the officers had gone to the trouble of collecting this transport it was taken away by the Higher Command and given to another unit. The same fate befell the second set of horses and waggons. The third was retained.

According to orders the Battalion entrained under the command of Lieutenant-Colonel Luther Watts, V.D., on the 13th August, at Lime Street Station, Liverpool. It was not known at the time whither the Battalion was bound. In the afternoon Edinburgh was reached, where there was considerable bustle on account of the departure of some regular regiments for the front. Crossing the Firth of Forth, the men saw with what activities the Naval Authorities were preparing for the reception of further warships. Dunfermline proved to be the destination of the Regiment, and on arrival supper was provided by some ladies of the town. The men were accommodated first in tents at Transy, and afterwards in billets in the Carnegie Institute, St. Leonard's and the Technical Schools and the Workhouse. The inhabitants of Dunfermline and district were extremely kind to all members of the Battalion, and almost every man had an invitation to visit newly formed friends nightly.

There were at this time not enough blankets in the possession of the authorities, so that an appeal was made which brought forth an ample supply of civilian blankets. Colonel Hall Walker, T.D., the Honorary Colonel, gave the Battalion £500 when it was at Dunfermline, which was expended on extra clothing and other comforts for the men. It was a very generous sum and proved of great value.

The usual training took place, and considering the circumstances a high standard of efficiency was attained. In October the Regiment proceeded by train to Tunbridge Wells, where it remained until it proceeded overseas.

The training here consisted of an early morning run followed later by a Battalion route march or field practice. Judged from later standards the training was not as intensive as it might have been owing chiefly to the facts that, unfortunately, no parade ground was available, and little, if any, assistance was afforded by higher formations. An occasional night alarm also ordered by higher authorities discomforted everyone and did little good. Recruits were sent to Sandwich for musketry, and the Battalion assisted in digging trenches, machine gun emplacements and other defensive works on the inland side of the canal, originally constructed by French prisoners during the Napoleonic Wars, and which skirted Romney Marsh. Half the Battalion—that is four companies—was sent to assist with the London Defences near Ashford, where the men learnt to construct what the Royal Engineers were pleased to call "Low Command Redoubts," and which were badly sited on forward slopes. The experience gained, however, proved very useful afterwards in France.

Parades at Tunbridge Wells finished early in the afternoon which afforded ample time for recreation. The townspeople were very hospitable and extended cordial invitations to the men, who availed themselves freely of them. At Christmas time the men fared sumptuously through the generosity and kindness of their hosts.

In January a company was sent to guard cables and vulnerable points at Birling Gap, Cuckmere Haven and Dungeness. Several other similar duties afforded diversions from the usual training programme.

While at Tunbridge Wells the greatest keenness was displayed by all. Officers were jealous of anyone who was lucky enough to be sent on a course of instruction. There were voluntary classes for the study of tactics at which the younger officers sedulously studied the principles of out-posts, advance guards, rear guards and so on. Everyone wanted to know more of his new profession. The thirst for knowledge was not adequately quenched as there were unfortunately, too few courses and too few instructors available.

Such an ardour possessed the men for the fight that in some it reached the pitch of fear lest they should arrive too late upon the battlefield and receive only a barless medal. Some actually wished to transfer to another unit so as to ensure getting out at once. When at last the anxiously awaited order came that the Battalion was to go "over there" one officer was overcome with exultation. His intense joy at being allowed to serve his King and country on fields more stricken than parade grounds was clearly marked. After many months of distinguished service in the field, he now rests peacefully at Montauban.

The few days immediately preceding the exodus of the Regiment were days of great activity and preparation. The affairs of the Battalion had to be completely wound up. The mysterious pay and mess books were completed and company cash accounts closed. New equipment was given out to officers and men, as well as wirecutters, revolvers and other necessities of active service. Field dressings were handed out—dark omens of what was now to be anticipated. The transport section received its full complement of waggons and limbers, together with its full number of mules, which proved to be equal to any which proceeded to France.

Under the impression that active service meant the end of the comforts of civilisation, officers provided themselves with supplies of patent medicine, bought small first-aid outfits and elaborate pannikins containing numerous small receptacles, which did not prove useful and were ultimately lost. Spare kit including Sam Browne belts was packed and consigned to the Depot. In anticipation of an early death many of the officers and men made their wills. This was encouraged by a rumour that the War Office had ordered a further 76,000 hospital beds to be prepared.

At the end of December, 1914, Lieut.-Colonel Luther Watts, V.D. took over the command of the Reserve Battalion at Blackpool, which had been formed late in 1914, and Lieut.-Colonel J.E. Lloyd, V.D., was gazetted to the foreign service Battalion.

Mention should here be made of the fact that shortly before leaving England the old eight company organisation was abandoned, and the new four company organisation adopted, and each new company was divided into four platoons. The change was exceedingly beneficial, as it would have been difficult in the field for a battalion commander to give orders to eight company commanders. More responsibility was thrown on the company commanders, who were at the time senior enough to assume it, and for the first time the subaltern was given a command. For the future he had his platoon which carried much greater responsibility than that previously attached to a half company. It was a fighting unit, and a separate body in which was reflected the work of a good commander.

The 12th March, 1915, was the day destined for the departure from Tunbridge Wells. One by one the companies, headed by a band kindly lent by one of the other units quartered in the town, marched through the streets for the last time. The greatest excitement prevailed when "D" Company, which was the last, passed through the streets just as the shops were opening. Farewells were waved, the troops were cheered, and for many this was their last look at the town which had afforded them every hospitality for the past few months.

Arrived at the station, the men entrained for an unknown destination, and there was some speculation as to which seaport it would be. It proved to be Southampton, from whence the men embarked later in the day for France. The excitement had to some extent worn off in the cool of the evening, and as the men had their last glimpse of England by means of the beam of the search-light, many thought of the happy homes they were leaving behind to which they would perhaps never return. The journey to France was uneventful, which circumstance was due largely to the protection afforded by the torpedo-boat destroyers and other units of the Navy.

CHAPTER II.
THE 1ST DIVISION.

Next morning the Battalion disembarked at Le Havre and marched to a camp at Sanvic. It was not to remain here long, and on the 14th the Battalion entrained to join the First Army. The train journey was long, and the men experienced for the first time the inconveniences of travelling in French troop trains, being crowded fifty-six at a time into trucks labelled "Hommes 48: Chevaux en long 8." Chocques was reached on the 15th and the men marched therefrom to billets in a village close by called Oblinghem. The Battalion was soon incorporated in the 2nd Infantry Brigade of the 1st Division, a mixed brigade consisting of four Regular battalions reinforced by two Territorial battalions. A few days were spent in Divisional Reserve at Oblinghem during which time all the officers and several non-commissioned officers were sent to the trenches at Festubert or Richebourg for instruction by the Regular battalions which were holding the line.

At Oblinghem the men learnt for the first time what French billets were like and experienced the insanitary conditions prevailing on the small farms and the draughty and dirty barns. Looking around the countryside all seemed quiet and peaceful. The ploughman ploughed the fields, others sowed and the miners went to their daily tasks as usual. At times it was difficult to realise that the firing line was within a few miles, but the boom of the distant guns and the laden Red Cross motors indicated the proximity of the fighting. A lot of old ideas as to the rigours of a campaign were lost, and warfare in some respects was found not to be so bad as had been expected. Wine and beer at any rate were plentiful, though the potency of the beer was not quite sufficient for the taste of the older men. Other regiments, lent officers to give a helping hand in organisation and training. Company messes for officers were formed, as anything in the nature of a battalion mess was impracticable.

The men soon learnt that the estaminets were the equivalent in France of the public houses at home, and thither they repaired in the evening to spend their time. Many good young men who had never taken a drop of the more invigorating liquors learnt that soldiers drank them, and the cause of teetotalism began to wane.

On the 24th a move was made to Les Facons, a straggling village outside Bethune. Here on quiet nights one could easily hear the fusillade in the trenches while the distant gun flashes lit up the night sky. The terrors of the trenches were coming nearer.

Early in April the various companies were attached each in turn to another battalion in the Brigade, and went into the line for instruction in trench duty at Port Arthur by Neuve Chapelle, and it was here that the first casualties were sustained. It is claimed that the first shot fired by the Battalion killed an enemy sniper. The men soon learnt the duties that fell upon them as a consequence of trench warfare: the early morning stand-to, the constant vigil of the neutral ground between the lines, and the imperative necessity of keeping one's head low. Hitherto the men knew little of the nature or use of guns, but now glimmerings of the mystery surrounding artillery fire soon dawned. The men learnt the natures of German shell, and the difference between shrapnel and high explosives and what targets the enemy generally selected. Facts like these were explained to them by the "real soldiers" of the Regular units to which they were attached. On relief the Battalion marched back to Oblinghem once more, where it stayed a week or two, and later in the month took over a portion of the line at Richebourg St. Vaast where it was subjected to a very heavy artillery bombardment on the 1st May.

The military training of the men can be said to have been complete as regards pre-war standard, but the war had introduced the use of two new instruments of death. One was gas, the other the bomb. A primitive form of respirator was given out in consequence of the use by the Germans of chlorine at the Second Battle of Ypres. Instruction was given in the use of bombs, of which the men had hitherto no knowledge. In those days the bomb first in use was the jam-tin bomb. The men were taught how to cut fuses, fix them into the detonator, attach the lighter and wire the whole together preparatory for use against the enemy. Jam-tin bombs were soon discarded for the Bethune bomb, and there was no regular bomb until much later, when the use of the Mills bomb became universal. The Hairbrush and Hales bombs were also studied in addition to the Bethune. A few also received some instruction in a rather primitive form of trench mortar.

In April, Lieut.-Colonel Lloyd, V.D., was invalided home, and in his stead Major T.J. Bolland took over the command of the Battalion.

THE BATTLE OF AUBERS RIDGE

The disastrous enterprise of the 9th May was the first major action of the war in which the "Ninth" took part. Shattered at its inception, the whole attack soon came to an end. The lack of high explosive shells and the consequent failure of the British artillery to destroy the enemy wire entanglements were probably the main causes of the holocaust that took place on that day. Though one of the biggest disasters the British arms sustained throughout the war, it was scarcely noted in the newspapers, and would seem to a casual observer quite insignificant compared with the sinking of the "Lusitania," which had taken place some days before, although in the battle it is believed that the 2nd Infantry Brigade lost a bigger proportion of men than had ever been previously known in warfare.

On the 8th May, the Battalion took up its battle position in rear of the Rue du Bois at Richebourg l'Avoué, and there awaited the attack on the morrow. The detail that obtained in battle orders of later dates was wanting, in view of the fact that greater responsibility was in the early days placed upon Commanding Officers. The Battalion was to support the attack as the third wave. The flanks were given and in the event of an advance the Battalion was to keep Chocolat Menier Corner on its immediate right. The fight commenced with an ordinary bombardment of forty minutes chiefly by field pieces, which according to the text book are primarily intended not for bombardment but for use against personnel. A battery of heavy howitzers was also in action. The ordinary bombardment was followed by an intense bombardment of ten minutes.

At 5-30 a.m. the Battalion advanced to the third line of trenches immediately in rear of the Rue du Bois, and several losses attributable to machine guns and shells were sustained. At 6-0 a.m. the Battalion was continuing the advance to the support line when the 2nd King's Royal Rifles asked for immediate support in the attack. The Battalion therefore passed over the support line and quickly reached the front line. The advent of a fresh unit made confusion the worse confounded. The trenches which afforded little shelter were filled with men, and the enemy was using his artillery freely. Machine guns in profusion were disgorging their several streams of bullets. Communication trenches had been blotted out. Despite the lessons of Neuve Chapelle there was no effective liaison between artillery and infantry as the telephone wires were soon cut, and as a consequence the inferno was intensified by the short firing of the British artillery, a battery of 6-inch howitzers being the chief offender.

Numerous casualties had been suffered, and among them was the Commanding Officer, who was killed. The command then passed to Major J.W.B. Hunt, who decided that it was useless to attempt to assault the enemy position without further artillery preparation, as the enemy's barbed wire was practically intact, and the only two gaps that were available were covered by enemy machine guns. A report on the situation was made to Brigadier-General Thesiger, and instructions were received that on no account was the Battalion to leave the front line, and it was to hold the same against a possible and probable counter attack by the enemy.

At 10-0 a.m. the Battalion was ordered to prepare to take part in a second attack to be launched at 11-15 a.m. Half an hour later a further order postponed the second attack until 12-30 p.m. Thousands had failed to take the objectives in the early morning, and it was unlikely that hundreds would succeed in the afternoon. This attack was ultimately cancelled, and at 4-0 p.m. the Battalion was withdrawn. A further attack was delivered in vain at 4-30 p.m. by other regiments in the Division. Though the Battalion unfortunately accomplished little, it sustained almost a hundred casualties, but it was fortunate in that it escaped the same fate as befell four of the Battalions in the Brigade which were almost annihilated. The battle from almost every point of view was a dismal failure, and the rate of casualties was perhaps the highest then recorded. It was during the 4-30 p.m. attack that the men were privileged to witness one of the most magnificent episodes of the war, which was the advance made by the 1st Battalion Black Watch and the 1st Battalion Cameron Highlanders. This was carried out with parade-like precision in face of a most withering rifle and machine-gun fire, out of which scarcely half a dozen of those brave fellows returned.

Relieved in the evening, the "Ninth" marched to Essars and the next day to billets at Bethune, and it was not until the 20th day of the month that the Battalion was again in line, this time at Cambrin. It had now come under the command of Major F.W. Ramsay, a regular officer from the Middlesex Regiment. The remainder of the month of May and the month of June were spent at Cambrin and Cuinchy, this latter place being renowned even in those days for its minenwerfer activity. The Cambrin sector had good deep trenches made by the French pioneers, which were strong, well timbered and comfortable. This was the first occasion the Battalion occupied trenches as distinguished from breast-works. Hitherto the nature of the ground had made trenches impossible. The trenches at Cuinchy were in front of a row of brickstacks, and in consequence of the water-logged nature of a portion of the front were only dug three feet down, and a sand-bag parapet was built; the trenches were not duckboarded, and were in consequence wet. Around each brickstack was built a keep, and this was garrisoned by a platoon in each case. Every time an enemy projectile hit a brickstack large quantities of broken bricks were scattered as splinters which multiplied the killing effect of the shell. In this sector there was considerable mining activity. The mine shafts, of which there were about three per company frontage, were each manned by two men who acted as listeners. As the front lines were only about twenty-five yards apart there was a considerable exchange of grenades.

No cooking was allowed in the trenches, as the smoke which would have been occasioned by cooking would only have encouraged enemy fire. Therefore ration and hot food parties had to go four times a day along a communication trench called Boyau Maison Rouge, one and a half miles long, and which was not duckboarded. After heavy rain it became very muddy, and the men cut down their trousers which led to the adoption of shorts throughout. Hosetops were improvised by cutting the feet off socks and later they were bought. The colour ranged at first from light heliotrope to flatman's blue, but later was standardized as salmon pink. The expense of providing these hosetops was a heavy drain on any available funds, but fortunately friends of the Battalion came to the rescue.

On relief from the Cambrin trenches on the 7th July the Battalion spent a little over a fortnight in Brigade and Divisional Reserves at Sailly Labourse and the Faubourg d'Arras in Bethune respectively. On the 25th it was in line at Vermelles. This sector was quiet except in that portion which was opposite the Hohenzollern Redoubt, from which huge aerial torpedoes were fired.

August was spent doing tours of duty in Annequin and Vermelles. During the last tour in Vermelles the whole Battalion assembled every night in no man's land and successfully dug under fire jumping-off trenches for the forthcoming operations, the casualties being comparatively few, owing to the speed with which the men dug.

During the first three weeks in September, the Battalion was out of the line and spent most of the time at Burbure, a quiet little village outside Lillers, where the men enjoyed a period of peace well removed from the battle zone. The training was devoted almost entirely to the practice of the attack preparatory to the impending fight.

During the summer a horse show took place in the First Division, and the "Ninth" secured all the prizes for mules, the first prize for a field kitchen and two jumping prizes, thus obtaining the second place in the Division for the total number of marks gained. This was a signal honour for a Territorial unit, and perhaps came as a surprise to some of the Regular soldiers, who thought that they were "the people." This demonstrated the fact that though the Battalion had but a few months' experience of active service, it had soon accustomed itself to the rigours of warfare, and that the transport section at any rate had attained a high pitch of efficiency. The horse shows which were held from time to time as occasion permitted provided diversions and did much to maintain a high standard of efficiency in the first line transport.

Improvements had been effected in the organisation of the Regiment since its advent to France. Clothing and food became more plentiful and the latter was better cooked. Efforts were made to improve the comfort of the men in billets. Proper sanitation was rigorously observed. Officers were encouraged to display the greatest solicitude for the welfare of the men, and the cumulative effect of these measures resulted in improved morale.

THE BATTLE OF LOOS.

For three weeks in September the Battalion practised the attack in Burbure, which it left on the 20th. Before leaving Burbure an amusing incident took place. The Battalion had paraded and was ready to move off. Suddenly two young women who were watching dashed into the ranks, embraced two of the men, kissed them with resounding smacks, and then disappeared in the gloom. The consternation of the two men caused great amusement to all. The "Ninth" moved up by stages, marching via Lapugnoy and Verquin, to its battle position in trenches by Le Rutoire Farm, which it reached on the 24th. The Battalion and the London Scottish formed a body called "Green's Force," to which was given as a first objective the German front line trenches in the vicinity of Lone Tree, as this objective was left uncovered by the diverging advance of the 1st Brigade on the right and the 2nd Brigade on the left.

In the grey light of the morning on the 25th September the British guns opened with a furious fire after many days of artillery preparation. The great battle had begun. For some time, and according to orders, the Battalion remained in its position. It was not to advance before 8-0 a.m. At this time the men left the assembly trench to move over the open to the front line. The enemy machine gunners had the range, and several were wounded almost on leaving the trench. The advance was made by sectional rushes, each section seeking what cover there was. Those who were wounded while actually advancing in many cases received slight wounds, but those that were hit while lying down were generally killed, as the bullets struck them in the head or traversed the vital organs for the length of the body. It required a courageous heart to advance seeing one's comrades thus desperately wounded or lying dead. The shell fire was not heavy, and few casualties were attributable to it. Lieutenant-Colonel Ramsay led the attack in person, and he was easily recognisable by the wand which he carried. One of the Battalion machine guns was pushed forward about 2-0 p.m. and under the covering fire it afforded the advance was continued. The advance had been slow and losses were severe, but at 3-30 p.m. the men had succeeded in establishing themselves in one line about a hundred yards from the German trenches. A few minutes afterwards the Germans surrendered, and between three and four hundred prisoners were taken. They chiefly belonged to the 59th and 157th Infantry Regiments. A harvest of souvenirs was reaped by the men, many of whom secured the then coveted Pickelhaube helmet. The prisoners were sent to the rear, and the

Battalion continued the advance and ultimately established a line on the Lens-Hulluch Road. It is to be observed that the Battalion was the only one that got its field kitchens up to the village of Loos on the first day of the battle. At 4-0 a.m. next morning the Battalion was withdrawn to the old British line. Later in the day it moved forward to the old German trench system as reserve in the continued operations, sustaining several gas and shell casualties. On the 28th September the Battalion moved back to Mazingarbe, as the men thought, for a rest. They were soon disappointed. At 7 p.m. on the same day orders were received to take up a position at the Slag Heap or Fosse at Loos, known as London Bridge. At 9-0 p.m. the Battalion left its billets in a deluge of rain and marched back to the line in splendid spirits in spite of the fatigue resulting from the recent fighting. It was relieved from the trenches on the 30th September, and after one night spent in the ruined houses of Loos went to Noeux-les-Mines for a few days to re-organise and re-equip.

On the 7th October the Battalion returned to the front line which was alongside the Lens-Hulluch Road to the north of Loos. The trench had evidently once been the ditch on the side of the road. It was very shallow, and it was decided to deepen it the next night as the men were too tired after their long march. This was a good resolution, but it was not carried out. The enemy commenced next morning about half-past ten with heavy shell fire. In the afternoon it became intense and an attack seemed imminent. There was no shelter in the shallow trench, as there had not been sufficient time to make any dugouts. The men could do nothing but wait. Minutes seemed hours. The shelling appeared endless. So terrific was the enemy fire that it was doubted by the artillery observers in rear whether any of the front line garrison was left alive. All who might be lucky enough to escape physical destruction would at any rate be morally broken. The Germans who had concentrated in the Bois Hugo attacked about 4-30 p.m. They were repulsed by rifle and machine gun fire, and it is gratifying to know that two of the Battalion machine guns caught the enemy in enfilade and executed great havoc. So exhausted were the men that the Battalion was relieved that night and taken to the neighbourhood of Le Rutoire Farm.

Acquitting themselves with a noble fortitude, the stretcher bearers—whose task was, perhaps, the worst of all—remained and toiled all night in evacuating the trenches of the wounded. To stretcher bearers fall the most trying duties in war, but in accounts of battles little mention is made of their efforts. While the fight is on they share all the dangers of the private soldier, and often they have to remain when the others are relieved to finish their duty. The terrible sights of open wounds, bodies that have been minced by shell splinters, torn off limbs, dying men uttering their last requests, are enough to unnerve the bravest men. The stretcher bearers nevertheless continue with their task, well knowing what fate may soon befall them.

For the second time in a fortnight the 9th King's had been called upon to play an important part, and worthily had the men acquitted themselves on each occasion.

The following letters were received by the Battalion and show the value of the good work done:—

To G.O.C., IV. Corps.

This was a fine performance and reflects the greatest credit on all ranks.

I particularly admire the splendid tenacity displayed by our infantry in holding on to their trenches during so many long hours of heavy shell fire, and the skill with which they so gloriously repulsed with bomb and rifle the enemy's most determined onslaught.

Our gunners, too, must be complimented on their timely and accurate shooting. And lastly the Commanders, from General Davies downward, deserve praise for the successful combination of the two arms, for the handling of their units, and for the well-judged advance of the supports to the aid of those in the fire trenches.

I am very glad to hear of the great deeds of the 9th Battalion Liverpool Regiment on the 8th October. They have proved themselves most worthy comrades of the 1st Liverpools who started with me from Aldershot and have consistently fought like heroes all through the campaign.

Please convey my very hearty congratulation to all concerned and to the 1st Division, in which I am proud to see the determined fighting spirit is as strong as ever, in spite of heavy losses.

D. HAIG,
General,
Commanding 1st Army.
10th October, 1915.

To 1st Division.

In forwarding Sir Douglas Haig's remarks, I desire to endorse every word he says, and to congratulate the Division on the well deserved praise it has received from the Army Commander. I hope before long to see them personally and to speak to them on parade.

H.S. RAWLINSON,
Lieut.-General,

Commanding IV. Corps.
11th October, 1915.

1st Div. No. 604/2 (G).
To 2nd Infantry Brigade.

The General Officer Commanding wishes to place on record his appreciation of the steady defence made by the 2nd Infantry Brigade against the German attack yesterday afternoon. He especially wishes to commend the soldierly qualities and discipline displayed by the 9th Liverpool Regiment and the 1st Gloucesters, which enabled them to endure the heavy shelling to which our front trenches were subjected, and there to meet and repulse with great loss the German infantry attack.

The result of yesterday's attack again proves how powerless the enemy's artillery is against good infantry, properly entrenched and the superiority of our own infantry over that of the enemy at close quarters.

The General Officer Commanding wishes to record his appreciation of the good work done by the artillery in support of the infantry.

H. LONGRIDGE,
Lieut.-Colonel,
General Staff, 1st Division.
9th October, 1915.

The above remarks were communicated to the men, and they were all very proud of the achievement of their unit and that it had so highly distinguished itself in the defence of their country. For a few days the Battalion remained in support, sending forth working parties each night for the battle that was still continuing.

On the 13th October the 1st Division attacked the village of Hulluch. An intense barrage was directed against the enemy trenches in the early part of the afternoon, and after a discharge of cloud gas an attempt was made in vain to reach the enemy trenches. The 9th was held in close support, ready to exploit any success that was gained, but, unfortunately, the attack was a total failure. The Battalion came in for some very heavy retaliatory shell fire.

On the 14th October the Battalion was taken out of the line and marched to Noeux-les-Mines, where it entrained for Lillers. Here the men were accommodated in houses in the centre of the town in the vicinity of the Church and the Rue Fanien. The billets were good, the parades not severe, and several of the officers who were well quartered felt to some extent the comforts of a home. The training area was near Burbure, where the Battalion had trained for the battle. Many faces were missing that had been present at the jovial little gatherings that had taken place before the battle, and the survivors wondered at times who would be wanting at the next divisional rest.

As the parades were not onerous, there was plenty of time for recreation. Concerts were arranged in the local concert hall at which the latent talent of the Battalion came into evidence. Leave opened, and the prospect of a trip to England was cheering to those who expected one. The rest at Lillers was pleasantly spent and it was a long time before the men enjoyed a similar holiday.

On the 15th November the Battalion paraded on the Church Square and then marched to Houchin, a particularly dirty little village, where a week was spent. From there it went to Brigade Reserve in the mining village of Philosophe, in which, though very close to the line, a few civilians still remained. Butter, milk and other articles of food could be obtained from the French shop-keepers, and English newspapers could be bought in the streets the day after publication. It was a fairly quiet place, though one's hours were punctuated by the intermittent firing of a battery of 4·7 guns in the colliery in rear, which fired over the billets.

One of the Regular battalions of the 3rd Infantry Brigade was too weak in numbers to do trench duty, and the 9th had the honour of replacing it, and on the 26th November the Battalion found itself once more in the front line and in exactly the same position as the one in which it had so signally distinguished itself on the 8th October.

Snow was lying on the ground and it was freezing hard. Henceforth the men were to know the hardships of a winter campaign. There were no deep dugouts and there were not sufficient shelters for the men to sleep in. During the course of the winter, exposure alone killed some. Ever since the battle the Loos sector had been very active, especially on Sundays, and the trenches and alleys which led up to them were in a very wet condition. The numbers lost in the recent fighting had not been made up, and "C" Company, the weakest, had a trench strength all told of only 67 officers and men.

The relief from the front line on the night of the 29th November was particularly severe. Following the frost came rain on that particular day, and the relief was carried out on a very black night in a steady downpour, and everyone was quickly wet through. The trenches filled with water and the men had first to wade through deep sludge and then over rain-sodden ground ankle-deep in mud. The men's clothes became caked with the mud from the sides of the trench, which increased the weight to be carried.

During the tours of duty in this sector the paucity of the numbers and the length of the communication trenches made the difficulties of food supply very great. Behind the front line in the Loos sector was a devastated region extending backwards for over two miles. There seemed a big gap between the front line and any form of civilisation. Usable roads were wanting, so that the transport could not approach near to the Battalion. Consequently each company had to detail its own ration party of twenty to twenty-five men, and these would assemble just after dusk and wander along Posen or Hay Alley back to the vicinity of Lone Tree, and there pick up the rations and water from the transport wagons. The communication trenches contained a lot of water and caused great hardship to those men who were not fortunate enough to possess gum boots. These ration fatigues lasted from three to five hours, after which the men had to continue their trench duties. Each man cooked his rations as best he could, in his own mess tin; this meant that he did not get a hot meal which was so badly needed in the intensely cold weather.

In this sector there was a great shortage of water. Washing and shaving were impossible, and at times there was not enough to drink. On one occasion a man was known to have scraped the hoar frost off the sandbags to assuage his thirst, and some drank the dirty water that was to be found in shell craters.

At this time there was a great danger of a gas attack, and it was customary to have a bugler on duty in the front line to sound the alarm when gas was seen coming over—a scheme which was scarcely likely to be efficacious, for in a few moments he would have been gassed himself. Each man had two anti-gas helmets—one with a mica window, and the other with glass eyepieces and a tube through which to breathe out, and which was known later as a P.H. helmet. There were Vermorel Sprayers here and there in the trench, which were entrusted to the care of the sanitary men. Instruction was given from time to time in anti-gas precautions, but viewed from a subsequent standpoint these defensive measures were not good.

Steel helmets were in possession of the bombers, who were then called "Grenadiers," and wore little red cloth grenades on their arms. These helmets were called "bombing hats," and regarded as a nuisance. Each man of the Battalion had a leather jerkin and a water-proof cape, and the majority had a pair of long gum boots.

There was only one Verey light pistol in each company, and this was carried by the officer on duty. There was no special S.O.S. signal to the artillery. Telephonic communication from the front line existed, and this was freely used. It was not known at the time that the enemy had evolved a means whereby he could hear these conversations. To prevent an illness known as "trench feet" each man had to grease his feet daily with whale oil, which was an ordeal on a bitterly cold day in wet, muddy trenches. With such meticulous care was this done that the Battalion had not more than three cases of trench feet during the whole of that winter—a circumstance which reflects much credit on the men. The defence scheme at this time was to hold the front line in the greatest strength available, and the supports were rather far away. The system of echeloned posts had not yet been developed. Machine guns were kept in the first trench and on account of the intense cold had to be dismounted and kept by lighted braziers to keep the lubricating oil and water in their jackets from freezing. The entanglement in front was very poor and consisted only of one fence.

When not in the line the Battalion rested at Noeux-les-Mines or Mazingarbe. At this latter village Christmas Day was spent. Companies were told to make their own arrangements for providing the men with a good dinner on this day. The officers provided the funds and the difficulties of supply were overcome through the aid of Monsieur Levacon, the French interpreter attached to the Battalion. Pigs and extra vegetables were bought; apples and oranges came from somewhere. After great exertions a few barrels of beer came on the scene. Christmas puddings came from England. The school at Mazingarbe made an excellent dining room for two of the companies and through the kindness of a Royal Engineer company in the village the officers were able to secure the necessary timber to improvise tables and chairs. The dinner was a great success and contributed not a little to the good feeling which existed between officers and men.

The next day the Battalion returned to the line. Though not known at the time this was to be the last tour of duty with the 1st Division. Early in January the truth became known that the Battalion was to leave the Division, and on the 7th it proceeded by train to Hocquincourt.

In the 1st Division it had had the honour of serving alongside some of the most illustrious regiments of the Regular Army. The example set by these famous regiments was readily copied, and in some respects emulated, and it is not untrue to say that none of these Regular battalions assumed an air of superiority, but displayed a sense of admiration that Territorial soldiers could have so quickly learnt the profession of war. So good was the human material in the Battalion that, in the space of a few months spent on active service, a body of men picked in a desultory fashion from various trades and occupations was quickly formed into an entity which was able to take its place alongside experienced units of the Army.

The Regiment had already won its laurels at the Battle of Loos. Its glorious achievements were known in Liverpool. It was a Battalion to which all its members were proud to belong. The fame of a military body is a bond of unity which those who have not been soldiers can scarcely understand. The reputation of one's regiment is a matter of personal pride. It is a kind of cement which holds it together at all times. The old spirit soon permeates the newcomers, the recruits become imbued with the spirit which led the veterans to victory, and so it was with this Battalion.

CHAPTER III.
THE 55TH DIVISION.

The West Lancashire Division was formed in the Hallencourt area under the command of Major-General H.S. Jeudwine, and given the number 55. The Battalion entered the 165th Infantry Brigade in this Division. This brigade which was commanded by Brigadier-General F.J. Duncan, was entirely composed of Liverpool battalions, namely, the 5th, 6th, 7th, and 9th King's. In the Brigade the officers and men had the pleasure of meeting friends they had known at home in Liverpool, comrades with whom they were destined to serve for the next two years, principally in Artois and Ypres. Friendly rivalry soon sprang up between the various battalions in the Brigade which made for efficiency and put all on their "mettle." Everyone naturally believed that his was the battalion par excellence, not only in the Brigade but in the whole Division.

The 9th was first billeted in Hocquincourt, a little French village near Hallencourt. Viewed from a distance the village looked picturesque, with the red tiled roofs of the houses contrasted against the sombre winter sky, but a closer inspection revealed a different picture. The houses were rickety, the billets poor, and the conditions insanitary. So backward were the peasants in agriculture that they still adhered to the use of the old-fashioned flails for thrashing corn. The Battalion moved on the 20th January to Mérélessart about two miles away, where better quarters were found particularly for the Battalion headquarters, which occupied a somewhat pretentious chateau replete with all modern conveniences including baths, which were very unusual in private houses in the war area.

Here the Commanding Officer, Lieutenant-Colonel Ramsay, D.S.O., left the Battalion on his promotion to the rank of Brigadier-General. Before he left he made a speech to the men and published the following "Farewell Order":—

On relinquishing command of the Battalion to take over command of the 48th Infantry Brigade, the Commanding Officer wishes to express his regret at leaving the Regiment, which he has had the honour of commanding for the last eight months, and his gratitude for the loyal way in which all ranks have supported him.

The Commanding Officer is very sensible of the fact that the excellent work done by the Regiment has gained for him his decoration and promotion.

Later in the war he received promotion and commanded the 58th (London) Division as Major General.

While at Mérélessart the usual training took place. There was little work done as a complete unit not much attention being paid to tactical work. A rifle range was at the disposal of the Battalion on which the companies were able to fire a few practices and so keep up their musketry.

It is worthy of remark that of the officers serving with the companies at this time approximately two-thirds were subsequently killed during the course of the war, while the survivors were almost all wounded at some time or other.

Early in February orders came along to the effect that the Division was to go into line, and on the 6th February the Battalion left Mérélessart and marched to Longpré where the night was spent, and the next day it reached Berteaucourt-les-Dames. A few days were spent here, during which Major C.P. James took over the command of the Battalion, and afterwards it marched via Doullens to Amplier, and after a night's rest in some huts there it reached Berles-au-Bois the next day. En route it passed through Pas, where there was a steep hill which presented such difficulties to the transport section that they remembered it when they returned in two year's time. At Berles-au-Bois the men were billeted in the ruined village. This was the first experience the Battalion had of a really tranquil front.

This village lay within a mile of the front line, and it seemed uncanny to be so near the enemy and yet to hear so few shots fired. Indeed it was almost too good to be true. The unit did not take over the defence of this area, and orders came soon that on the 15th the Battalion was to take over a sector on the Wailly front, where it was to relieve a battalion of the 81ième Régiment Territoriale. Accordingly very early in the morning of that day the Battalion marched to Monchiet in sleet and rain under cover of darkness along roads which in daylight were exposed to the view of the enemy, and on arrival the short day was spent in endeavouring to get dry. Monchiet later became the location of the transport lines and Quartermaster's store.

WAILLY.

Having sent an advance party to General Xardel's headquarters at Beaumetz to effect liaison, and to meet French guides, the Battalion paraded towards evening, left Monchiet, picked up the guides en route and marched to Wailly. The day had been one of blizzards and the night of the relief was black and wet. Added to these circumstances was the difficulty of understanding the directions of the Frenchmen, the Battalion's knowledge of their language being not very extensive. Towards midnight, thoroughly drenched, hungry and weary after a heavy day, the men were ultimately put in their proper stations, some in the village and others in the trenches.

From the appearance of the houses Wailly had been a prosperous farming village lying within a short distance of Arras. Agricultural implements of the latest manufacture were in evidence, and these could only have been bought by peasants with some capital. This village was to be the Battalion's home for the next five months. The Battalion first did a month alternating in position between the front line and the village. For some days while in the front line the Battalion was in touch with the 27ième Régiment d'Infanterie, which had a sentry post in its area composed of men from one of the companies who readily fraternised with the fantassins. This regiment belonged to a division of the French Active Army, and in consequence its efficiency was of a very high order. Nowhere had anyone seen trenches so well revetted and so neatly constructed as those occupied by this French regiment. The trenches stood out in marked contrast to those actually taken over by the Battalion, whose former occupants, the French Territorials, had left them in a very bad condition.

The trenches had not been revetted or duckboarded, and during the first month of the Battalion's occupation there was a good deal of snow, and when this melted the sides of the trenches commenced to crumble, making them very muddy at the bottom. In consequence of this mud they became almost impassable. For the men doing trench duty the conditions were bad enough. The man on post had to stand on the fire step for hours in damp clothes, shivering in the freezing cold, knowing that when his tour of duty was over all he could look forward to was the cold damp floor of a dugout on which to rest his weary body. For the ration parties the conditions were almost worse. The meals were cooked in the field kitchens in the village, and fatigue parties to carry up the meals were found by the support company which was in a trench called by the French the Parallèle des Territoriaux. Many of the men will never forget the innumerable times they trudged heavily laden with a dixie of tea or stew through the mud in the tortuous communication trenches Boyau Eck, Sape 7, and the Boyau des Mitrailleuses. At times these trenches became so muddy that on one or two occasions reliefs had to be carried out over the top under cover of darkness. It was risking a good deal to line up a whole company outside the trench a few yards in rear of the front line, knowing that an enemy machine gun was located about a hundred yards away, and that the machine gunner might fire an illuminating flare at any moment, and so expose the men to his view.

It was during the first tour at Wailly that Major C.G. Bradley, D.S.O., assumed command on the 29th February.

After having done a month in the Wailly sector, the Battalion was taken on the 14th March for a week in Brigade Reserve. Though the Battalion only got into billets at 1 a.m., after a four mile march, a working party had to be found at 8-30 a.m. for work on a Divisional show ground, which was a place where model trenches were dug to show the uninitiated how things ought to be done. Tasks like these were regarded as onerous by the men, who were led to expect some period of rest when not in the advanced positions.

After a few days in Beaumetz the Battalion returned to Wailly, and until June continued to do three tours of duty at Wailly, two in the front line and one in the village, to one in Brigade Reserve at Beaumetz, the whole cycle lasting a month.

The enemy having in line opposite the 78th Landwehr Regiment, the sector was very quiet, though the British did what they could to liven things up in the way of artillery shoots and indirect machine gun fire at night on the roads behind the enemy lines.

The general defence scheme at first was not very elaborate. Three companies manned the front line with one in support. Great attention was paid to bombing posts, and the defence scheme always contained a plan for a counter attack by the bombers, who were organised as a separate section, working directly under the orders of the Commanding Officer. They were given simple schemes and exercises in counter-attack while in the trenches. For example the non-commissioned officer in command of a squad would be told that the enemy had entered a particular sector of the trench. He would then block the trench or deliver an imaginary counter attack along the trench with the object of dislodging the fictitious enemy, as the case might require. The companies were trained to take shelter in the dugouts in the event of a heavy bombardment and immediately on its cessation to re-man the front line. In the village when the Battalion was in support it held three centres of resistance known from right to left as Petit Moulin, Wailly Keep, and Petit Chateau. Wailly Keep was a fortified farm on the fringe of the village, with loop-holed walls and the adjacent roads barricaded. It was a relic of the French defence scheme and was sound.

The strictest precautions were taken against a gas attack. Each man had two P.H. helmets which he had to keep with him at all times. Moreover, sentries were instructed how to recognise gas and sound the alarm immediately they noticed enemy gas. Large cartridge cases from the guns were used as gas gongs, and Strombos horns were installed so as to spread the alarm quickly should occasion arise. This was a much better scheme than the one in which the bugler was to sound the alarm. As the lines were near there was some danger of a flammenwerfer attack, so the whole Battalion was taken on the 17th March to a demonstration, and shown what to do should such an attack take place. One Lewis gun was given to each company in place of the machine guns which were taken away from the Battalion, and the Stokes mortar made its appearance in the trenches. This was an over-rated weapon. Its range was very limited and it was soon out-distanced by similar German weapons. Its bombs were essentially for use against personnel at a range when rifles would have been cheaper and more efficacious. Its bombs were not heavy enough for use against earthworks, and wrought little damage on trenches. Its use and its ammunition supply entailed large carrying parties which robbed the companies of the men and sapped their energy.

In May steel helmets were made part of every man's equipment, and a square green patch on the back of the tunic became the Battalion distinguishing mark. The steel helmets were the means of saving many lives, and were covered with the same material as the sandbags were made of, for purposes of camouflage.

One night early in April a patrol consisting of a corporal and a private was sent to examine and report on the enemy wire in front of a particular sap head. At this point there were only seventy yards or so between the British trench and the enemy sap heads, which were swathed in a dense mesh of barbed wire. There were but few shell craters, little artillery fire being directed on the front line when the lines were close owing to the danger of short firing; and the grass being short there was little or no cover. The night had been very quiet. Scarcely a rifle shot had broken the silence. The patrol must have made some noise, and so aroused the attention of the enemy sentry in the sap head who fired an illuminating flare. The light betrayed the presence of the patrol to the enemy, who opened fire and wounded both of the men. Afterwards the enemy kept firing illuminating flares and maintained a lively rifle and machine gun fire, so that any attempt at rescue was impossible. At dawn the enemy put up a flag of truce and a party of them came out and gently lifted the wounded into their own trench. It was noticed that the enemy were wearing the old blue uniform of the German Army instead of the feldgrau uniform, and that they carried tin canisters in which they had their gas masks. This rescue was accomplished at great risk to the enemy as they did not know that the British would refrain from firing; and the incident proves that at any rate there were some among the Germans who would do the honourable thing. When the Battalion was at Ypres about a year afterwards a letter came saying that the graves of the two men had been found with an appropriate inscription in the German language.

In this sector there was much work to be done. The trenches, which were in a state of decay after the frosts and rains of the winter, had to be duckboarded and revetted. Besides sandbagging the front line the Battalion, in conjunction with the relieving unit, the 7th King's, constructed a new support line known as Parallel B., in which was accommodated, when it was complete, a portion of the front line garrison. The wire needed attention as well. The French had covered the front with a chain of *chevaux de frise*, but this was not considered a sufficient obstacle, so that concertina wire and "gooseberries" had to be put out in front of the *chevaux de frise*. The wiring parties had a very difficult task, as they had to work about forty yards away from the enemy, who were often engaged on similar work. Also the men had to work in front of the *chevaux de frise*, and they would have had great difficulty in getting back to their own lines should they have been surprised by the enemy. Besides this, innumerable rifle racks, bomb stores, machine gun emplacements and other works of a similar nature were completed. In addition to this the men had to form large carrying parties to carry large elephant sections and other material to the Quarry for use by dugout construction parties of the Royal Engineers.

At this period the trench discipline attained a high standard as the men had been together for some months and free from heavy casualties, and it is well here to digress for a while and record what trench duty really meant. "Stand to" would be at say 3-30 a.m., shortly before dawn. At this time all would man the parapet and wait until it became daylight. The rifles, ammunition, gas helmets, and feet of the men would be inspected by the platoon officer. This generally took about an hour and a half. Afterwards the men not actually on duty would wash and shave. Shaving in the trenches was made compulsory in March, as it was thought that it kept the men from deteriorating and would prevent any tendency to slovenliness. There was little water for such a purpose, and consequently it was particularly arduous in a muddy trench, and it is doubtful whether the benefits derived were worth it. Breakfast would take place between six and seven. Afterwards the men got what sleep they could during the day, but they were constantly interrupted by sentry duty, meals, shell fire, and occasionally a fatigue. The activity of night replaced little by little the tranquility of the day. Towards sunset came evening "stand to" and more inspections. After nightfall patrols would go out, and wiring parties for the renovation and repair of the wire, ration parties for the food, and working parties to keep the trenches in good condition would be detailed. The men got no sleep at night, and in fact very little at all. Trench duty was exacting and exhausting from a physical point of view alone, but to this was added the continual attrition of numbers on account of shell and rifle fire.

In May the weather was glorious and the face of the countryside assumed a pleasant aspect. The trees were in full leaf. Wild flowers in profusion adorned the trenches, and larks in numbers hovered in the clear blue skies above the trenches and sang sweetly in the early mornings. The sunsets viewed from the front line were particularly beautiful. The lines of trees on the Beaumetz-Arras road became silhouetted black against the skyline, reddened by the setting sun, which produced a wonderful effect.

As the summer advanced the front became more active. Shell fire increased, and the British artillery, having a more liberal supply of ammunition, expended it more lavishly than had been formerly the case. In July the Battalion left the sector immediately in front of Wailly and took over that in front of Blaireville Wood, which was held by the enemy.

On the 28th June a series of raids took place on the Divisional front, which were covered by a discharge of cloud gas. A party from the Battalion took part in the raid, and two officers were able to enter an enemy sap but they did not manage to secure any prisoners. The junior of the two officers was unfortunately killed, being shot through the head. In retaliation for the raids the enemy brought up, on the 2nd July, what was called a "Circus" consisting of several 150 m.m. and 210 m.m. howitzers on railway mountings, with which he utterly destroyed the front line trenches for a distance of two hundred yards, blew in several mined dugouts, and inflicted heavy casualties on "D" Company. In some respects this was the heaviest and most destructive bombardment that had been endured by the Battalion up to this time, though it was not so prolonged as that of the 8th October, 1915.

On the 8th July, after five months continuous duty in the forward zone, the Battalion went into Divisional Reserve at Gouy-en-Artois, where the Battalion was housed in hutments close by the Divisional School.

The Somme Battle had commenced, and there was every likelihood of the Division being called upon either to attack on the front it already held or as reinforcements. In consequence the Battalion, which had had very little training for the past five months, turned its attention to practising the attack in some cornfields near the hutments it occupied.

The attack was henceforth to be made by successive waves of men and to each wave was assigned a particular objective. Following these attacking waves there came what were called "moppers up," whose task was to deal with any of the enemy who might have hidden in dugouts and so escaped the attention of the attackers. Recent lessons of the Somme Battle costing many lives had brought about the necessity for the institution of moppers up. The rear waves were also to act as carrying parties. One man had to carry a coil of wire, another a spade, another a screw picket, and so on. The reason for this was, that when the enemy trenches had been captured, the enemy might cut off all supplies by means of an intense barrage on no man's land, and it was necessary for the attacking troops to have sufficient material at hand to enable them to put the captured positions into a state of defence immediately, and thus be able to resist a counter-attack. Model trenches were marked out and much good work was done in the attack practices that took place. Large drafts arrived and the Battalion was soon in excellent form. The cleanliness and smart appearance of the men while in the village drew forth the special praise of the Divisional Commander.

At Gouy a Battalion concert party was formed, and a concert was given in a large barn which formed part of the Divisional Canteen. The doctor composed some verses for the occasion in which there was plenty of local colour.

In June a Divisional horse show had taken place at which the Battalion again distinguished itself. "C" Company cooker again took first prize in the Division, and the Battalion secured the second place for the total number of marks gained.

The days spent in this sector were comparatively pleasant. The front had been quiet, and although the work was arduous casualties were few, and leave was regular. In the light of later experience the time spent in Wailly was very comfortable indeed, and during the next two months many wished they could return.

THE BATTLE OF THE SOMME.

About the 20th July the Battalion left Gouy-en-Artois for the scene of battle. To begin with this meant a three days' march to the entraining locality. The first day the Battalion got to Sus St. Leger where the night was spent, and by the end of the second day the Battalion was at Halloy. On the third day, after a long tiring march in hot weather along dusty roads, the Regiment marched into Autheux. After a few days here the Battalion entrained late one evening for the front, and next morning it detrained at Méricourt. The first sight that the men beheld on quitting the train was a prisoners' camp, in which were many Germans, living evidence of the activity a few miles in front. The Battalion was billeted in Méricourt for two days. Here there was every indication of activity. Having been on a quiet front for several months the men were not used to the whir of a busy railhead. All manner of vehicles, guns, and other impedimenta of war were in evidence, and everyone was surprised to see some of Merryweather's fire engines, which were probably required for pumping purposes.

On the 29th the Battalion left Méricourt for what was known as "The Happy Valley," outside Bray. During the march the soldiers saw a mile or two away an enormous column of smoke ascend. Something terrible had taken place. An ammunition dump must surely have been blown up. It was not a very pleasant prospect for those who were new to that kind of thing.

The mystery of the column of smoke was never clearly elucidated. The Happy Valley was scarcely correctly named. The weather was exceedingly hot, there were no billets, and consequently the men had to bivouac. The Valley had one great drawback; there were no wells in the vicinity from which water could be drawn. Owing to this shortage, the water-men had a very onerous task as water was obtainable only at Bray, and thither the water carts had to go, making as many journeys as possible during the day, to obtain water for the thirsty troops. The Battalion in this locality was in touch with the French, from whom the officers managed to secure some of the French ration wine which proved very acceptable.

On the 30th the Battalion moved to a place by Fricourt, and pitched a camp which it left two days later for a bivouac area by Bronfay Farm, near Carnoy. From this place the officers went forward on reconnaissance. They saw for the first time Bernafay and Trones Woods, which then had achieved great notoriety. To the neighbourhood of these woods the Battalion sent forward night working parties. Only with the greatest difficulty did these parties get to their rendezvous, and little work was done on account of the intensity of the enemy shell fire.

In the evening of the 3rd August the Battalion paraded and marched towards the fighting, leaving behind a small percentage to form a nucleus should all its fighting personnel perish. The march was wearying. The enemy guns were active, the weather hot, and packs heavy. After a long trudge the Briqueterie was reached, a dangerous and dreaded spot, for it was periodically swept with shell fire. At last the companies got to their allotted stations in the reserve trenches. Many had not yet experienced the terrors of heavy shell fire, which by its very nature was intended to produce an unnerving effect. The next day started fairly quietly. On the right the men could see what was known as Death Valley. This was rightly so called. Being obscured from the enemy's view, it was a covered means of approach to the infantry positions in front, and afforded at the same time cover for the guns. On this account it was never free from shell fire, and was littered with corpses of men and horses.

In the afternoon the Battalion had to take over the front line in the neighbourhood of Arrow Head Copse in front of Guillemont. Passing along Death Valley the Battalion got caught in heavy shell fire, and sixty casualties took place almost immediately. It required a stout heart to march cheerfully forward when seeing one's companions who had gone a little in front coming back on stretchers, or lying dead alongside the path.

When the two leading companies arrived at Arrow Head Copse they manned trenches varying in depth from a few inches to three feet, which afforded little protection against shell fire. The dead, many of whom belonged to the Liverpool Pals Brigade, were visible lying stark and numerous on the battlefield. The weary desolation, and the unmitigated waste of equipment, clothing, and life passes all description. This was the Somme battlefield, of which one had heard so much. To those who had seen much of the war, the thought came that nothing could be worse than this.

The next day was a day of incessant shell fire on both sides. On the British side it was the bombardment prior to the attack on Guillemont. The fire was terrific. The terrible concussions of the high explosive shells assailed both ears and nerves, and kept up a pall of dust over the trenches. The whizzing and swirling of the shells was incessant. Some whined, others moaned, and others roared like express trains. Light shells passed with an unearthly shriek. It was useless taking any notice of the lighter shells. They had come and burst before one realised what had happened. The heavier shells, particularly those that were timed to burst in the air, were very trying, and when they burst over Trones Wood the noise reverberated through what remained of the trees, and so became extraordinarily intensified. To expect the explosions of the shells knowing they were on their way and to hear them coming, not knowing whether they would be fatal or not, was the worst part of the ordeal. Such a condition of turmoil and torment must have been meant by the words of Dante in his description of Hell.

"La bufera infernal che mai non resta."

Every now and then a man was hit. Those killed outright were perhaps spared much agony, and the wounded were lucky if they reached the aid post alive. Many got shell shock which affected men in different ways. One would be struck dumb, another would gibber like a maniac, while a third would retain possession of his reason but lose control of his limbs.

For two days in the sultry heat the Battalion endured the terrible strain of this awful shell fire, the men receiving no proper food and water being unprocurable. Then the Battalion was relieved and taken into support, where three or four days were spent, and on the 10th two companies moved to the Maltz Horn position. The next night the two remaining companies moved up. The devastation in the neighbourhood of Cockrane Alley was worse than at Guillemont. Here the men witnessed the full terrors of the stricken field. Living men dwelt among the unburied dead. Booted feet of killed soldiers protruded from the side of the trench. Here and there a face or a hand was visible. Corpses of dead soldiers with blackening faces covered with flies were rotting in the sun, and the reek of putrifying flesh was nauseating. Added to this the heat was overpowering, the artillery was firing short, and there was little or no water obtainable.

The Battalion was in touch with the French, and there were a few Frenchmen in the trenches with the men. On the 12th August the French attacked with great success and captured the village of Maurepas.

Between the two armies there was a wide broken-in trench running from the Allied towards the German lines. For some time before zero the Allied artillery kept up an incessant barrage on the German lines. The shells fired by the French were noticeable by a much sharper report. At zero the French attacked on the right of Cockrane Alley, advancing at a run in small groups of from eight to twelve men, and they got a good distance without any casualties. Then one by one the Frenchmen commenced to fall, and on reaching the enemy line the French company immediately on the right of the Battalion met with strong resistance. None came back and it is thought that almost every man perished. Meanwhile the two companies of the Battalion attacked in waves on the left of Cockrane Alley. They got eighty or ninety yards without difficulty, when the enemy opened a heavy machine gun fire, and the ground being convex the attackers formed a good target. The Commander of the right company who led his company from the right so as to be in touch with the bombers in Cockrane Alley, though twice wounded, still continued the advance until he was shot dead. His example was emulated by the Company Sergeant Major who perished in similar circumstances. Meanwhile the bombers were endeavouring to work their way down Cockrane Alley. The trench became shallower, and on reaching a road it disappeared. As the bombers emerged on to the road they were shot down one by one. The enemy then turned their machine guns on to Cockrane Alley, and raked it with fire until it became a shambles. Most of the men of the two companies were casualties, and many were killed. A few stragglers who were able to take cover in shell craters managed to return later under cover of darkness.

What became of the wounded lying out between the lines was never known, as any attempt at rescue was impossible. As most of the stretcher bearers with the companies were themselves incapacitated through wounds the rapid evacuation of the wounded even in the trenches was impossible, and moreover the aid post at Headquarters was under heavy artillery fire, so that it was only at great risk to the bearers that the wounded could be cleared at all from the trenches.

For the French the day had been very successful. They had captured Maurepas, but for the Battalion it was a total failure. However, the work done earned for the Battalion the praise of the Corps Commander, expressed in an order published the next day, which was as follows:—

The Corps Commander wishes you to express to the Companies engaged last night his admiration, and that of the French who saw them, for the gallant and strenuous fight they put up.

Had the ravine been captured by the French, there is no doubt our objective could have been realised.

13th August, 1916.

On the 13th the Battalion was relieved and the men, tired out, slowly wended their way down Death Valley to Maricourt, passing many corpses, and then to the bivouac area near Bronfay Farm they had left about ten days before. Many who had marched away in the fullness of their health and strength did not return. The next day a short move was made to Ville-sur-Ancre, one of the few villages which contained a shop. Shortly afterwards the Battalion moved by train to Ramburelles, not far from the coast. Of all the villages the Battalion had ever visited, this was perhaps the most insanitary. The men lived in barns almost on top of manure heaps, and in consequence of the heat the number of flies was great. Baths of late had been very few and consequently the men suffered considerably from lice.

Arduous training was the order of the day. Seven or eight hours each day were devoted to work, while what the men most needed was rest. They were exhausted after their late experience, and they were overworked by the excessive training. Many were further weakened by the fact that septic sores were very prevalent owing to the insanitary conditions among which the men lived.

At this period the Battalion routine orders, which were supposed to be issued early in the afternoon were, for some unknown reason, always received very late in the day and sometimes after ten o'clock at night. As the Company Commanders had then to issue orders it meant that much unnecessary waiting and work was caused.

At Ramburelles so as to evade the heat of the day the Battalion paraded at 7 a.m. for a four-hours' parade, and then left off until late in the afternoon. This scheme worked well only in theory. A lot had to be done out of parade hours, which meant that the officers and men were very much overworked. Sunday brought no respite. The Sunday previous to leaving the place, the men were engaged on a work of supererogation until 8-30 p.m., digging bombing trenches which were never used.

While at Ramburelles seaside leave was granted to some of the officers, who were able to spend two or three days away from the Battalion and enjoy for a while the comforts of a seaside town. One or two, acting in the belief that the Battalion would not return to the fight for some time, postponed their trip, and on the very day that they arrived at Delville Wood they remembered that that was the day they should have been basking in the sun at Le Treport. Such is the folly of procrastination. On the 28th August the command devolved on Major P.G.A. Lederer, M.C., as the Commanding Officer had been evacuated sick. On the 30th August the Battalion marched by a tortuous route to Pont Remy, where it entrained and arrived next day at Méricourt. It eventually was installed in close billets at Dernancourt for a few days.

On the 4th September the Battalion marched to Montauban. On the march Major H.K.S. Woodhouse took over the command, and the officers were introduced to him during the dinner halt. Montauban was not a very pleasant place, particularly as the weather was rainy, and as the companies were distributed among the field guns they came in for considerable shell fire.

On the 7th September the Battalion moved up to the front positions between Delville Wood and High Wood. The shell fire in this area was terrific. The enemy guns never stopped firing day or night at the means of approach to the Battalion's position along the side of Delville Wood. At night the Battalion had to send working parties into the neutral ground between the lines to dig what were somewhat incorrectly known as strong points. When these were finished they were garrisoned by a platoon in each case. The small garrisons of these strong points were quite cut off during the day as no movement was possible on account of snipers. Food and water could only be brought up at night, and were a man wounded he would have to remain without attention until darkness. A prisoner was taken belonging to the 5th Bavarian Regiment, which showed that the Bavarians were in line opposite.

On the 9th there was a big attack by the British. The 16th Division attacked on the right in front of Delville Wood, and the 1st Division on the left, and consequently the Battalion was in the very centre of the fight. The garrisons of the strong points being cut off as they were, did not receive news of the attack. Suddenly in the afternoon after a comparatively quiet morning the artillery on both sides became very active, both the British and German artillery developing intense barrages. To the men in the strong points this presaged an enemy attack, and the order was given to be ready to fire the moment the enemy should come into view. The members of these small garrisons knew there would be no hope for them, as they would soon have been surrounded and annihilated, and most probably all of them bayoneted. Fortunately the attack was by the British and these eventualities did not arise. The Battalion was relieved during the next two days and went into reserve at Buire-sur-Ancre. After a few days here it moved to a bivouac area at E. 15 a., outside Dernancourt. Though this was some considerable distance behind the front line the enemy forced the Battalion to evacuate this area by firing at it with a long-ranged gun. In the evening there was a cinema show in the open, at which were shown pictures of the Somme Battle. It was very strange to see the soldiers keenly interested in the pictures of what shell fire was like when there were actual shells falling about half a mile away, and they had been shelled out of their camp that very afternoon. The British Army had made a successful attack on the 15th September, and on the 17th the Battalion went into line again at Flers, where two miserable days were spent in an incessant downpour of rain and very heavy shell fire. On relief it came back to the transport lines at Pommier Redoubt.

On the 23rd the Battalion paraded, leaving behind its surplus personnel and moved up to Flers for the attack. Orders were received the next day that the attack was to take place on the 25th, and that zero was to be at 12-35 p.m. The objective allotted to the "Ninth" was from Seven Dials to Factory Corner, which meant an advance of 1,000 yards. At 7-30 a.m. the barrage commenced and lasted for hours, and increased in intensity as the moment for the advance drew nearer. At zero the Battalion advanced in four waves, the distance between the waves being 100 yards. The first wave had to keep close to the creeping barrage of shrapnel. Of the last wave scarcely a man survived, as it came in for the enemy barrage which the leading waves had escaped. The bombers took an enemy strong point and fought their way along Grove Alley and got to work with the bayonet, inflicting many casualties on the enemy and taking several prisoners. This was the first experience the men had of advancing under cover of a creeping barrage of shrapnel and the first occasion that they saw tanks in action. The attack was a great success and reflected no little credit on the Battalion. Everyone of the Headquarters personnel present will remember the Advanced Headquarters being blown up and the signallers and runners sustaining many casualties. During the same evening two companies of another unit came to the trench occupied by Headquarters. They tried to enter the trench at the same spot and crowded close on each other. At this time the enemy suddenly dropped four 5.9 shells among the crowded men. Next morning forty-seven dead were counted.

The next day the Battalion was relieved, and by small stages the remnants of the companies made their way to Buire-sur-Ancre. This was the Battalion's last time in action on the Somme, and it presented a very changed aspect to its first arrival on this battlefield. Companies were reduced to the size of platoons, and platoons to sections or less. During the battle about 650 casualties had been sustained, including fifteen officers dead. This was a large incision into the fighting strength, and it was a long time before these losses were made up.

For the Battalion the Somme Battle with its terrible holocausts, incessant shell fire and continuous slaughter, was at an end, but there was no respite for the weary soldier. There was to be no rest or period for recuperation. The Regiment was ordered to Ypres immediately. Tired and exhausted, the men were taken out of the Somme inferno, having lost many of their comrades, and with weary bodies and heavy hearts they faced the prospect of the untold terrors of the fatal city of Ypres.

The journey to Ypres was long. First the Battalion entrained at Méricourt in the afternoon of Sunday the 1st October. At midnight the men detrained at Longpré and marched to Cocquerel, arriving at 3 a.m. the next day. The men then bivouacked until reveille at 6-30 a.m. At 8-30 a.m. the Regiment was again on the march to Pont Remy, where it entrained for Esquelbecq, where it arrived at 9-30 p.m., and marched to billets at Wormhoudt. Two days were spent here, and this afforded the men the rest they so badly needed. The state of the Battalion can be gauged from the fact that at Wormhoudt only one company commander had a subaltern.

YPRES.

On the 4th October the Battalion entrained on a light railway, and soon reached Poperinghe, where it remained until darkness and then entrained on a broad gauge train at Poperinghe Station for Ypres. It was a new experience for the men to be in a train and yet within range of the enemy's artillery. The personnel detrained just by the railway station at Ypres and went into billets close by. Little could be seen of the city in the dark. Stillness pervaded the area that night, and after the Somme Battle the quietness was uncanny.

The next day the men had an opportunity of seeing the city that had suffered so much in the war. It must have been subjected to many a tornado of shells, for there was not a single house untouched and very few had roofs. A few shells fell in the Square during the morning, but that was all. To the men it was a great relief to be in a quiet area after such a place as the Somme. Ypres was not as bad as had been expected.

The trenches were to be taken over at once. The officers reconnoitred the line during the afternoon, and towards evening the Battalion paraded and marched along the Rue de Stuers, the Rue au Beurre, past the Cloth Hall, through the Square, and the Menin Gate towards Potijze. Afterwards it took over the sector from the Roulers Railway to Duke Street with Headquarters in Potijze Wood. Four days only had elapsed since it had left the Somme railhead. This area was to be the Battalion's battle station for several months to come, and many times were the companies to repeat the journey they had just completed. It was to take part in two big battles in the vicinity and add greatly to its honours and leave many of its members entombed in soldiers' graves in what was to be perhaps the biggest graveyard of its kind in the world.

The Ypres sector was very quiet, but there was every danger of a gas attack, and the Battalion received the strictest warnings from the relieved unit, which had lost many men two months before through inattention to precautionary measures. The first night that the Battalion went into the line there was an alarm, but as the wind at the moment was in a safe quarter its falsity was immediately recognised. The men at this time had only the then out-of-date P.H. helmet. These helmets were changed in the course of a week or two for the more efficacious box respirators, which remained with slight modifications until the end of the war as the soldiers' protection against enemy gas. The enemy artillery was very quiet, and obviously the British had the artillery ascendancy, and it was surmised that this was attributable to the fact that he had removed his artillery to the Somme. The minenwerfers were active and so were the enemy snipers. After a tour in the line the Battalion repaired to Ypres. A few days afterwards it went to take over the "L" defences at Brielen, with Headquarters in Elverdinghe Chateau. Only one tour was done here and the Battalion then returned to Ypres. Until January it did three tours of duty in the line, either in Ypres itself or the front line to one in reserve at Brandhoek.

While in the front line the routine was practically the same as at Wailly, but the conditions were different. In the Salient it was not possible to dig deep trenches as the land was so low lying that water was met on reaching a depth of about two feet. Trenches were not feasible, so it was a case of breast-works. The defences therefore consisted of sand-bag revetments held in position by wooden frames over which expanded metal had been spread. These frames were called "A" frames or "Z" frames. The former were used for preventing narrow ways from staving in, and the latter were to face sand-bag walls. They were not easy to use and the men had to learn how to fix them, and their employment entailed many long and tedious carrying parties. The breast-works were divided into fire bays by traverses which were situated every few yards. These fire bays, which were all numbered, had firing platforms made of wood or well-revetted sandbags. The parapet was sufficiently high to give good command over the ground in front. During the winter it silted down and in many places it became not even bullet-proof. The parados was fairly good, though in many places there was none at all. For shelter the men had small recesses like dog kennels in the parapet or parados; these were usually roofed by a sheet of corrugated iron and were very small, uncomfortable, and infested with rats. There were not sufficient shelters to accommodate all the men, and the surplus had to sleep as best they could on the firing platform with only greatcoats as coverings.

The men had endured much and many were war weary. They were tired of fighting, and their former enthusiasm had cooled, especially as there was no immediate prospect of a rapid termination of the war. Among those who stood to arms in the whizz-banged trench in the cold raw hour of dawn were many who had given up assured positions—skilled mechanics, master printers, clerks, university men, solicitors, and others of several professions and callings who had sacrificed their various situations and appointments, and whose wives struggled on a very meagre separation allowance. Fully aware were they also that while they were manning the trench as infantrymen and receiving as remuneration a miserable pittance, munition workers in England were receiving excessively high wages for congenial work and enjoying freedom from all discomfort and danger of the trenches.

The water-logged ground between the British and German lines was pitted with shell holes and overgrown with rank grass and weeds. Numerous trees lopped of their branches were still standing, while many others were lying on the ground. Exactly half way across to the enemy lines were the remains of what had been a moated farm, which was a favourite objective of patrols. Railway Wood, which was situated on slightly higher ground on the right of the Battalion's sector, was a minehead and in consequence the scene of much activity. At one time there had been a wood, but so intense had been the artillery fire that not a single tree or trunk higher than three or four feet was left standing. Almost every afternoon, about 4-30 p.m., the usual trench mortar "strafe" would commence, and would last for an hour or so. A few months later Railway Wood became a scene of much mining activity, and mines and camouflets were sprung either by the British or the Germans almost daily. In the Battalion area there was situated what was known as Number 6 Crater, a deep mine crater half full of water, and said to be then one of the largest in France. In the vicinity of this crater there were some overhead traverses to prevent the enemy snipers from enfilading the trench, probably constructed after several casualties had been incurred.

Company headquarters were close to the front line, and never consisted of anything more than a small shelter. The cooking was done in cook-houses in the company areas, fatigue parties being detailed to bring up rations and water in petrol tins. Battalion headquarters were housed in dugouts in the wood adjoining the White Chateau at Potijze, in front of which was a large cemetery. While in Ypres itself three companies were billeted in the cellars of the gutted houses in the neighbourhood of the Boulevard Malou, which was a better class district once inhabited by the more wealthy citizens. Headquarters and one company were housed in the cellars of the Ecole Moyenne, which was erroneously called the Convent. These billets were not bad, though in many cases damp.

For the companies there was a parade in the morning, and every evening several working parties paraded at the Convent, and marched out afterwards through the Menin Gate for work in the Brigade area. The biggest working party numbered 100. It moved off at 5-30 p.m., drew shovels, picks, and gum boots at Potijze Dump, and then worked until almost midnight in constructing Cambridge Trench. The work was inadequately supervised by the Royal Engineers, who left the task to a second corporal and a few sappers, and consequently little progress was made and most probably the trench was never properly completed. The men had their last meal at 4-30 p.m., and as a consequence they could not work with proper efficiency right up to midnight. After a while they became very tired and were unable to continue. As a considerable quantity of material was requisite to keep the trenches in repair, large carrying parties were necessary. These could have been to a large extent obviated had light Decauville railways been constructed, such as the Germans were discovered later to have been using.

For the comfort of the men there was a Divisional canteen near the billets in Ypres, and another in the Infantry Barracks. There was a recreation room in the Prison, where Church parades were held later. There were also baths in the Rue d'Elverdinghe, so that the men were able to keep clean.

During the day there was very little movement at Ypres, but at night this was different, as the transport lorries had to bring up stores and ammunition for the guns. They used to go through the city at a great pace for fear of being caught by the enemy shell fire, and it is interesting to record that on one occasion a complaint was made by the Battalion to the effect that the streets were unsafe at night on this account. This of course was in addition to the unsafety resulting from enemy fire.

When in reserve the Battalion was stationed at "B" Camp at Brandhoek, on the Poperinghe-Ypres Road. Here the officers and men were accommodated in very comfortable wooden huts, from which Poperinghe, with its shops and cafes, could easily be reached. Attention should be directed to the rigorous sanitary measures which obtained in this Corps, chiefly due to the insistence of the Corps Commander. Great progress had been made in this direction since the beginning of the war. Latrines and ablution places were kept scrupulously clean. All rubbish was cast into the incinerators, and billets had to be kept clean and tidy. On relief each unit had to obtain a certificate from the relieving unit to the effect that the billets had been left in a clean and sanitary condition. These measures, though rigid, were beneficial and kept down sickness to a large extent.

On Christmas day the Battalion was in Ypres, and one of the Churches in the Boulevard Malou was decorated, and proved a useful dining room, in which the men partook of a good Christmas dinner which was thoroughly enjoyed. After the meal the Commanding Officer ascended into the pulpit and treated the soldiers to an inspiring address, but it can be safely assumed that the men enjoyed the meal much more than the lecture.

The New Year was heralded by an intense bombardment by the British, and in anticipation of the enemy retaliation the front line was cleared, except for the officer on watch, and Lewis gun teams. The line was badly knocked about by the enemy fire, but was built up again by the Battalion in one night.

In January the first Divisional rest for ten months commenced, and it was spent by the Battalion first at "Z" Camp and then at Proven. The weather at this time was intensely cold, and as the men in "Z" Camp had only Nissen huts they suffered greatly in consequence. These huts were made of unseasoned timber, and large gaps appeared in the floors through which the cold east wind entered, reducing the temperature to a figure well below zero.

The first week or so was devoted to training. There was a fear at this time that the principles of open warfare might easily be forgotten during the long periods of stagnation in the trenches. Consequently exercises in open warfare were ordered by the Higher Command, and the Battalion carried out several tactical schemes, and also some night operations. These latter struck the men as rather unnecessary, as they had all been on night patrols in the neutral ground between the lines, which after all was what might be called the real thing. The other exercises were very beneficial, as were also the attack practices which took place.

At Proven the men discovered that the term Divisional rest was a misnomer. Reveille was before six, and in the dim light of the early morning, the men had to wash and shave in icy cold water in the teeth of a bitter east wind. There followed a meagre breakfast cooked on an unsheltered field kitchen in the dark, and often in the rain. The men paraded at seven, and went out on a working party for the rest of the day. Their tasks were to load earth on railway trucks and then off-load it after a short train journey, to serve as ballast for another portion of line that was in course of construction. The earth was frozen several inches deep and it was necessary to loosen it by means of a pick before it could be shovelled on to the trucks. Towards the evening the men returned, cold, weary and tired, to a draughty barn, with the dismal prospect of a similar day on the morrow.

For the officers there was a lecture by the Commanding Officer on a pamphlet recently brought out called "The Division in the Attack." The lecture took place every evening at 5 p.m. in the village school, and this meant that in many cases the officers were on duty for twelve hours continuously. During the day time there was also a Lewis gun class for the officers who were not on the working party, and they studied the weapon assiduously. While at Proven the Battalion was visited, while working on the railway, by Lord Wavertree, then Colonel Hall Walker, the Honorary Colonel, to whom the officers were presented. It seemed a long time since they had seen him last at Sailly Labourse, and his presence was very welcome to all the old members.

An outbreak of scarlet fever prolonged the Battalion's stay for a few days, but on the 23rd February it left Proven, detrained at the Asylum at Ypres and moved into billets at the Prison, with two of the companies in the Magazine. While in the Prison one of the officers facetiously remarked that it was a much better gaol than he had been used to, and observed that it was built on the panopticon principle. The next day the Battalion moved to its old haunts at Potijze, and resumed duties as before. During this tour Lieutenant-Colonel F.W.M. Drew took over the command in succession to Lieutenant-Colonel Woodhouse. At this time so short was the Battalion of officers that "D" Company had only one officer, who was the Company Commander, and as his company was disposed partly in a sector of trench known as X3, Potijze Defences, St. James' Trench and the Garden of Eden, he had a good deal to do.

On the 4th March a successful raid took place on an enemy post opposite to Number 5 Crater, in the vicinity of the Railway. The sentry post was in a sap head around which the wire had been cut up by shell fire. A shrapnel barrage was directed against the post for a few minutes, while the raiding party was waiting in no man's land. The barrage lifted suddenly, and the small raiding party rushed in and, taking the sentries by surprise, secured them as prisoners. On the 19th March the enemy successfully raided the Battalion, and unfortunately captured about ten prisoners. The plan adopted was ingenious. The night had been exceptionally quiet, when suddenly about half an hour before dawn the enemy opened with a barrage of all calibres on the sector immediately on the left of the Battalion, with the intention of diverting the attention of the British artillery to that sector. The enemy raiding party meanwhile was lying in no man's land. The enemy suddenly opened with a devastating fire on the Battalion's trenches for a few minutes, lengthened the range, and under cover of this barrage the raiding party entered and surprised the men in the front line. Orders had lately been received that the officer on watch was not to fire the S.O.S. signal to the artillery until he was sure that the enemy had left their trenches. But as it was dark he could not ascertain this, and consequently the signal was not fired. The Company Commander sent back the S.O.S. signal, but the message was not delivered through the foolishness of a signaller who was afraid to use the power buzzer, fearing that the enemy might intercept the message. The Germans left one of their men dead in the trench and another just in front of the parapet. This was an incident which had to be avenged, and soon the Battalion by means of two successful raids secured enough prisoners to equalize.

Towards the end of the month another raid was expected. To frustrate this the Commanding Officer decided to have a body of about sixty men lying in the middle of no man's land, in such a position that they would escape the enemy barrage and intercept the raiding party and take them by surprise. This was a sound scheme, but it was very exhausting for the men who had to lie for four or five hours on the frozen ground. Moreover, the anticipated raid did not eventualise.

The 13th March was the anniversary of the advent of the Battalion to France, and as the Battalion was then at Brandhoek, the sergeants invited the Commanding Officer and the remaining original officers who had landed at Le Havre with the Battalion to attend a smoking concert. The officers spent a short time at the concert, during which the usual eulogistic speeches were made.

About this time the platoons were reorganised in accordance with a training pamphlet that had lately been issued. Henceforth they were to consist of a Lewis gun section, a section of bombers, another of rifle grenadiers, and a fourth of rifle-men, and the men were taught the new formation to be adopted for the attack which was known as the "Normal Formation," one consisting of lines and waves of attackers.

In April, when the Battalion's turn came for a period in reserve, two companies had to remain in Ypres to assist the Royal Engineers with working parties, so that the personnel of these companies missed their period of rest. At this time one of these companies had its headquarters in a house in a terrace called the Place d'Amour. In the gardens of the houses a battery of field guns was installed, and there was another just close by. The headquarters of these two batteries were also in the Place d'Amour—one on each side of the infantry company headquarters. One morning the enemy decided to annihilate one of the batteries and commenced to fire ranging shots over the terrace. The artillerymen knew what was coming, and told everyone to leave the billets, but to uphold the honour of the infantry, the men refused to leave the billets until after the gunners had evacuated the position. They got away just in time.

On the 17th April the Battalion moved to the Ecole, a place outside the city on the east, which had apparently been a large technical school, and after a few days here it moved to Railway Wood sector where things were very active. After a tour here and a few days in reserve it returned to Potijze sector once more. On the 11th May a very successful night raid was carried out by two officers and forty other ranks on Oskar Farm. Under cover of a barrage two parties entered the enemy positions. Some Germans were found in a dugout, which was then bombed and six Germans surrendered. A small bombing party was counter-attacked by six Germans, and the sergeant in command shot three and bayoneted one, while the other two escaped. The War Diary states that on the way back some of the prisoners became unruly and were effectively dealt with, which means that they were killed. At least ten Germans were killed besides those in the dugout that was bombed. The prisoners belonged to the 1st Matrosen Regiment of the German Naval Division.

On the 17th May the Battalion went to Bollezeele, where it remained for a month. This was a clean, well-built village, where the men were very comfortable. The training ground was about an hour's march away, and so the Battalion paraded in the main street every morning with the drummers in the centre, and marched to the training ground where the companies were placed at the disposal of their commanders for drill and instruction. A meal was taken at noon and when the afternoon's work was done the Battalion reformed and marched back to billets. The weather at this time was very fine. Never had the men witnessed such beautiful blue skies, and scarcely a drop of rain marred the stay in the village. The Brigade sports were held early in June, and the Battalion did very well in the military contests, winning three out of four events, but unfortunately not quite so well in the others.

On the 11th June the Battalion left Bollezeele, and early the next morning arrived at Ypres, and immediately went to the usual sector at Potijze. As the shell fire in this area had become much more severe of late, to move troops through Ypres or even around it was done at great risk, and all were glad when the move was over.

By a chain of unfortunate circumstances, leave for officers had been very slow. In January it had been stopped as it was considered necessary for the officers to be with their men during training while out of line. Difficulties of transport brought about the closing of leave from January to June. It opened again in June, but as all could not go at once it happened that some officers did not get leave for nine or ten months.

After a few days in Potijze sector the Battalion sidestepped to the Wieltje sector. The tour here was characterised by intense enemy artillery activity. Heavy batteries constantly countered each other, and day and night were punctuated by cannonades of varying intensity. Ypres itself was shelled by the celebrated 420 m.m. Skoda howitzer. The enemy drenched the area with the old lachrymatory gas shells, as well as a new gas he had lately introduced known as "Yellow Cross" or "Mustard" gas. Bilge Trench came in for special attention, and on one day it was estimated that 1,200 heavy shells fell in its vicinity.

It was a time of great aerial activity also. Richthoven and his squadron visited the sector quite frequently—generally in the early morning—and fired machine guns at the men in the trenches. His squadron could be easily distinguished, as the bodies of the aeroplanes were painted red. Also they flew very low, and the anti-aircraft gunners did not dare to fire, leaving it to the infantrymen to defend themselves with Lewis guns as best they could.

During the tour in Wieltje the Battalion dug Hopkin's Trench in no man's land, under machine gun, granatenwerfer and rifle-grenade fire, which were the cause of several casualties. Fortunately there was a very good mined dugout at Wieltje containing many rooms which were lighted by electricity. The shelter it afforded reduced considerably the number of casualties that would otherwise have taken place, and it was a pity that there were not more like it.

Though very good work was done by the companies during these months of trench duty, it should be remembered that perhaps the most dangerous task was the bringing up of rations and water. Ypres was approachable from Poperinghe by one road only, along which came almost all the supplies for the troops in the Salient. From a point on the road called Shrapnel Crossing to the city it was within convenient range of the enemy artillery, and being well aware that the road was much used at night, the enemy subjected it to considerable fire, and caused casualties nightly. Once arrived in Ypres the Battalion transport had to pass the Square and the Menin Gate, which were well known danger points, where there was no cover, and then proceed to Potijze along a road that could easily be enfiladed by the enemy gunners. No matter how heavy was the enemy shelling there was no night on which the transport section failed to deliver the rations.

At the beginning of July the Battalion went to Moringhem to prepare for the great battle. This was a very small hamlet, and there must have been a great concentration of troops in the Pas de Calais, as this little place had to accommodate two battalions. The men were placed under canvas, and some of the officers lived in tents, while the remainder were accommodated in billets. The training was mainly devoted to the attack. The British and the enemy trenches were taped out on some cornfields, in propinquity to the hamlet, and the forthcoming attack was rehearsed time and time again by all the battalions in the Brigade. Great attention was paid to synchronisation of watches, and the immediate reporting of all information. Maps and aeroplane photographs of the ground were studied with meticulous care, and a model of the Battalion's sector over which it was to attack, showing Uhlan Farm, Jasper and Plum Farms, Pommern Castle, and Pommern Redoubt, was constructed outside the camp to explain the lie of the ground to the men. Tanks were represented by half limbers during these practices, and the shrapnel barrage by drums.

During the stay at Moringhem the officers were able to ride into St. Omer on one or two occasions, and there dine at the restaurants, where a welcome change in their usual menu was obtainable.

THE THIRD BATTLE OF YPRES.

On the 21st July the Battalion left Moringhem, and once more found itself at "B" Camp at Brandhoek. This was a very different place from what it had been during the winter, and being full of troops, the Battalion had only one-third of its former area in which to accommodate itself. Anti-aircraft batteries, tunnelling companies, transport lines, field hospitals, and observation balloons were everywhere.

The training was complete. Everyone knew the orders and it was merely a case of waiting for "Z" day, the day of the attack. On the 29th July, which turned out to be "X" day, the fighting personnel left Brandhoek, and moved to Durham Redoubt, an area just west of Ypres, where the men bivouacked for the night. The next day illuminating flares, iron rations, spare water-bottles, bombs, and maps were given to the men.

Though all knew the rôle of the Battalion and its allotted objectives, no one in the Battalion knew the extent of the attack, or which divisions were attacking, or what was to happen if all objectives were captured. It was believed that if the attack succeeded, there were other divisions in rear ready to exploit the success. Wild rumours began to filter through. One of the most prevalent was that eighty mines would be sprung at zero, and this was inspiring to all, and infused new courage into the men.

Towards evening the companies left the area, and slowly in the darkness moved via the Plaine d'Amour past the Dixmude Gate and the Dead End to Oxford Trench, where they took up a position and waited. This waiting was very unpleasant, as the enemy was obviously expecting an attack and shelled the whole area almost all night. There was little shelter, as the trench was shallow and wide, and several were wounded before the fight commenced.

The objective allotted to the Battalion consisted of a section of the enemy second line called the "Stutzpunkt" Line, comprising Pommern Redoubt (called "Gartenhof" by the Germans) to Bank Farm, known to the enemy as "Blucher." The distance of the objective from the Battalion's zero position was approximately a mile and a half, which was at that period of the war a big distance to be called upon to cover in one day.

Two hours before zero it became known that the artillery was firing gas shells on the enemy batteries, so that at zero the enemy would not be able to work their guns. The drone of the gas shells passing overhead, and the knowledge of this device on the part of the British artillery, was very reassuring to the waiting troops.

For a few minutes before zero all was tranquil, and the men were quietly waiting. Zero was at 3-50 a.m., at which hour it was quite dark. Suddenly there was heard the firing of an 18-pounder battery. It was a battery firing just a second or two early. There followed a deafening roar. All the guns had fired together, and their shells were racing across the sky. A sheet of flame covered the enemy trenches. The fight had begun. The men rose from their positions slowly and went over the top to the front line, where according to plan they waited twenty-five minutes. The advance then continued. They should have advanced in waves, but that was impossible over the shell-cratered ground, as the going over the churned-up earth was very difficult, particularly in view of the heavy loads the men carried. All cohesion was soon lost, and the men sauntered forward in little groups endeavouring as best they could to keep the proper direction. No one knew what was happening. After passing the enemy front line all danger from his barrage was over, but his machine guns were active, and every now and then a man dropped—in many cases not to rise again. At length the river Steenbeek was reached. Numbers were few and hopes of success were rapidly vanishing. How the fight had progressed on the right or left no one knew. In front was a strong position on the other side of the Steenbeek Valley, which turned out ultimately to be Bank Farm.

The enemy in the dim light was firing his machine guns and causing casualties, but with a final rush the men were in the centre of a German strong point. The companies were weak, one consisting of only a dozen men or so, and the Germans were in occupation of the position as well, and fired coloured lights to encourage the support of their artillery. They were dealt with by the bombers, and one sensible private, who soon used up all his available bombs found a store of German bombs, which he employed to advantage. About the same time another party of the Battalion captured Pommern Redoubt, while the 7th King's on the right got into Pommern Castle. In all about eighty prisoners were taken, which considerably exceeded the numbers of the men that first dashed up to the objective. The prisoners belonged to the infantry regiments of the 235th Division, and a few of them were artillerists belonging to the 6th Feldartillerie Regiment.

The taking of Pommern Redoubt was specially commented upon in the Dispatch of Sir Douglas Haig dealing with this battle, though the Redoubt fell much earlier than was therein stated.

Among the dugouts several things were found, such as field glasses, medical apparatus, rifles, bombs, and so on. In one was a store of bottles of aerated water. In another there was a store of rations which were ultimately consumed, and strange to relate, in one dugout there was a copy of a recent number of the "Tatler."

The position was consolidated, trenches were dug and manned by the men. A captured German machine gun was turned round and got into action. Four or five hours after the capture of the Stutzpunkt position another brigade continued the attack, but though the efforts of its members were successful at first they had in consequence of their exposed flanks to retire at nightfall, and the Battalion was then holding the line without anyone in front. Rain commenced to fall, and the ground having been churned up by countless shells, the whole area soon became dissolved into a morass of spongy earth pitted with innumerable shell craters half full of water. The trenches that had been dug soon filled, and the men were wet through. They were utterly exhausted, and some of them had to get what sleep they could, huddled up in these wet trenches, with their feet several inches deep in water.

Cooking was impossible, and it was only with the greatest difficulty that any food at all could be supplied to the men in the advanced positions. Added to this was the fact that the enemy artillery was exceedingly active, and the shells killed many in the exposed trenches. The British heavy artillery also fired short, which had a most demoralising effect on the men in front.

On the 2nd August it became known that the enemy intended definitely to recapture the Stutzpunkt line. The men were informed of this, and told to resist to the last. All available men were sent up from the transport lines to reinforce the men in front. These reinforcements suffered considerably from shell fire on the way up, but their advent inspired and cheered the weary men who had been through the whole fight, and whose rifles were in many cases so choked with mud as to be unserviceable. Towards midday the enemy developed a heavy barrage. He was about to attack, and everyone was waiting for the anticipated onslaught without fear, as all felt that any counter-attack would be repulsed with great loss. The S.O.S. signal and machine guns were ready, but the artillery observer saw the enemy first, and the artillery barrage of the British soon dispersed the attack.

Owing to the insufficiency of the number of surviving stretcher bearers, the evacuation of the wounded was exceedingly difficult. These were collected in a dugout at Bank Farm, where they lay for a long time after having received some slight attention. Two wounded Germans whom the stretcher bearers had been unable to clear were handed over to the relieving unit. The Battalion Aid Post was at Plum Farm, where the Medical Officer and his staff worked to the limit of their powers in attending and evacuating wounded.

Major E.G. Hoare, who was in command of the Battalion during the operation, wrote a poem which describes the conditions of the Ypres battle, and it is here given in full:—

THE VALLEY OF THE SHADOW.

31ST JULY, 1917.

Down in the valley the Steenbeek flows,A brook you may cross with an easy stride,In death's own valley between the rowsOf stunted willows on either side.You may cross in the sunshine without a care,With a brow that is fanned by the summer's breath.Though you cross with a laugh, yet pause with a prayer,For this is the Vale of the Shadow of Death.

Down in the valley was rain and rain,Endless rain from a dismal sky,But the valley was Liberty's land again,And the crest-line smoked like a Sinai.Rain that beat on the tangled massOf weeds and pickets and broken wire,And astride the stream was a brown morass,In the valley of water and mud and fire.

Down in the valley the barrage fell,Fountains of water and steel and smoke,Scream of demons and blast of hell,The flash that blinds and the fumes that choke.The mud and the wire have chained the feet,You are up to the knees in swamp and slime,There's a laugh when the crossing is once complete,But a setting of teeth for the second time.

Down in the valley the shambles layWith the sordid horrors of hate revealed,Tattered khaki and shattered greyAnd the splintered wrecks of a battlefield.Thank God for the end that is sure and swift,For the fate that comes with a leap and bound,But what if God leaves you alone to driftTo the lingering death in the pestilent ground?

Up on the slope was a line hard pressedBy bullets and shells and relentless strain,An enemy massing behind the crestAnd a trench that crumbled in fire and rain.Sleepless, shelterless, night and day,Drenched and weary and sniped and shelled,The word was given that come what mayThe line must hold, and the line was held.

But all who pass to the crumbling trenchMust go in the spirit that games with fate,With feet that stumble and teeth that clenchOver the valley of hell and hate.Over the knees in water and mud,Up to the waist if you miss the track,You shall know your path by the trail of blood,And silent figures shall guide you back.

Down in the valley the waters flow,You may jump the brook with an easy stride,They cross it in silence, they who knowWhat happened that day upon either side.In the voice of the brook are their comrades' tones,In the summer's breeze they shall feel their breath,For under the grass we have laid their bones,Here in the Vale of the Shadow of Death.[A]

[A] Copied by permission from "Dawn and Other Poems" by Lieut.-Colonel E. Godfrey Hoare, D.S.O. Publishers: Erskine Macdonald, Limited.

The Battalion was relieved on the night of the second-third, and the men drifted down in small parties through the mud to Potijze. Some hours were spent here, during which several casualties took place, as the enemy subjected the area to the fire of 8-inch shells. Towards evening the men were told to rendezvous at Vlamertinghe. There was no need to pay much attention to the means of getting there. That could be left to the men themselves. Everyone was ready to give them a lift, for their muddy appearance showed that they had just been in the fight, and consequently practically all arrived in motor lorries. At Vlamertinghe, rum was issued and later all embussed for the Watou area, which they reached shortly after midnight. After debussing there was a short march to billets. For some even this was too much, and about thirty were unable to walk, and had to be sent to hospital. The remaining men were put into billets, and at 4-30 a.m. the officers sat down to dinner, the first proper meal they had had for several days. Afterwards they lay down to sleep for six or seven hours.

What had been done by the Battalion during the last few days, at the commencement of the struggle for Passchendaele, was then perhaps the greatest achievement the Battalion had accomplished. Undoubtedly it had done well, and the following message was received from the Brigade Commander:—

To Officer lCommanding,
9th King's Liverpool Regt.

Will you please congratulate all ranks of your Battalion on the great gallantry they displayed during the recent operations? They not only captured all their objectives, but also helped other troops to capture theirs. The magnificent way in which they captured the position and held it against all counter-attacks makes me very proud to have such a Battalion in my Brigade.

L. BOYD MOSS,
Brigadier General,
165th Brigade.
4th August, 1917.

On the 6th August the Battalion was taken by train to Audruicq, and billeted near by in a hamlet called Blanc Pignon, where the next six weeks were spent. The troops were well housed in this place, which was very clean in comparison with the other villages in which the Battalion sojourned from time to time. Each man was given a new suit, deficiencies in kit were made up, and the companies soon began to resume their normal appearance. Leave opened, and it was possible for those who wished to have day trips to Calais, and one or two of the more fortunate managed to get seaside leave at Paris Plage or Wimereux. The time spent at Blanc Pignon passed without special incident, except that one night there was a bombing raid by which the Germans obviously hoped to blow up the ammunition dump which was in close proximity to the billets. Fortunately, although many were dropped, not one of the bombs was effective enough to explode the ammunition. During the raid a large Gotha aeroplane was caught in the beam of one of the searchlights, and this was the first occasion the men saw this particular type of machine.

Despite the training the men had undergone before the battle, there was a good deal of time devoted to field work, as in view of the experience gained and the lessons learned in the recent attack new tactics had to be evolved. Until the Third Battle of Ypres, the chief obstacles to the advance of the British had been the German wire entanglements. The fuses on the British shells had always permitted the shells to bury themselves to some extent before exploding. This meant that a crater was formed, and though the enemy wire in the immediate vicinity of the crater would be destroyed, the obstacle effect of the whole entanglement remained almost in its entirety. A new fuse which was known as No. 106 was introduced in 1917, by means of which the shells would explode instantaneously on impact, and the splinters would destroy the wire over a much bigger area than had formerly been the case. The artillery could now ensure the proper cutting of the enemy wire entanglements, and it had been anticipated that in the attack of the 31st July the troops would not encounter serious obstacles in the way of wire entanglements, particularly as they were to be supported by tanks. It is true the artillery had cut the wire, but several units had nevertheless been held up. The Germans had anticipated to some extent the British methods of attack and invented a system of defence to meet it.

The Commander of the Fourth German Army which was defending the Ypres sector, Infantry General Sixt von Arnim, was a commander of high standing, inasmuch as the British Higher Command had thought fit to publish some observations of his on the Somme Battle. In the Ypres sector he had adopted the plan of holding the forward zone with few troops well disposed in depth, with strong reserves in rear which could be used for an immediate counter-attack before the British could consolidate any positions they had won. His advanced troops were carefully echeloned in fortified farms, each strongly concreted and armed with several machine guns. The advantage of this scheme was that it afforded few definite targets to the British artillery, and gave every opportunity to the Germans to ambush and enfilade advancing British infantry. Tanks were of little avail against these block-houses, which in reality formed a belt of small fortresses which could only be overpowered one by one. At any rate they could easily break up the force of an attack, and inflict a large number of casualties at a small loss. The reserves could then be used to counter-attack the British before they had properly put the positions won into a state of defence. Such a method of defence was indeed a difficult obstacle to the advance, and its efficacy had been learnt at great cost in the last fight. This system of defence meant that new tactics had to be evolved to combat such a scheme. The German method of defence was explained in printed sheets and the explanations were retailed to the men. In the numerous tactical schemes and attack practices that took place the men were taught to encircle enemy strong points rapidly and close in on them. These exercises were supervised by the Divisional Commander in person.

While in this area another Divisional horse show took place, the third to which the Battalion had sent entries. It was rather a good show, and there was some very fine jumping, in which Belgian cavalry officers took part. The Battalion secured two first prizes for a water cart and limbered wagon, two second prizes and two third prizes. It obtained the third place in the Division for the total number of marks gained.

All good times come to an end and the 14th September was the Battalion's last day at Blanc Pignon. The occasion was marked by great festivities, and most of the men apparently consumed large quantities of beer. For this they could not be blamed as they were going into action, and might never survive to indulge so freely again. The next day the Battalion moved by train to Vlamertinghe, where the men bivouacked in the open, having for shelter large bivouac sheets.

The orders were that surplus personnel had to be left here, and all the officers who had taken part in the Battle of the 31st July were, with one exception, left behind. On the 17th the Battalion moved up from Vlamertinghe to Ypres, turned left at the Water Tower, skirted the Plaine d'Amour and proceeded along No. 5 Track to the neighbourhood of

Warwick Farm. The next day the Battalion headquarters and two companies moved up to Bank Farm and took over the front shell crater position. Though two big attacks had taken place since the Battalion was last in this area, the front line was approximately in the same place as when the Battalion had left it in the early days of August. A fortified farm called Somme had been captured, and that was about all. Hill 35 was still in possession of the enemy. The Battalion with its sister regiments in the Brigade was to succeed where others had failed.

The Battalion held the shell crater position from the evening of the 18th, and it was obvious that the enemy expected an attack as he searched the whole area with heavy artillery fire at dawn on the 19th.

The two remaining companies moved up after nightfall on the 19th. It commenced to rain and the difficulties of placing the men in their proper places were great. The night was black and there was nothing by which one could locate oneself. After several hours a tape was placed along the line of shell craters to serve as a jumping off mark along which the men were duly aligned.

The *rôle* of the Battalion was to capture Hill 35 and Gallipoli, which was a strongly fortified centre of resistance in such a position, situated on rising ground, that it commanded a large area to the north. After its capture other units in the Brigade were to pass through the Battalion and continue the attack. The distance of the attack by the Battalion was from four to five hundred yards, and it was to be made in four waves, a company to each wave. It was anticipated that though the position might be fairly easily captured the enemy would make a desperate effort to dislodge the attackers.

The attack was evidently anticipated, as the enemy shell fire for a few minutes before zero was particularly heavy. Meanwhile the British artillery maintained a silence in which the gunners were able to prepare for the impending barrage. Zero was at 5-40 a.m., and at that time suddenly there opened an enormous crescendo of fire from the British guns, together with a machine gun barrage, which latter some attributed erroneously to the enemy. At this time it was fairly light, and one could see from a hundred and fifty to two hundred yards, quite light enough to enable the German machine gunners to inflict many casualties.

Owing to the fact that the men had to jump off from shell craters, and many were anxious to advance quickly so as to evade the enemy shell fire, and that there was some mixing of units, the waves were somewhat confused. The German artillery was ready and intensified its fire. The enemy machine gunners opened fire at once and the attackers began to fall almost as soon as the attack was commenced.

On the right of Hill 35 the Germans had manned a derelict tank and could not be dislodged. Even though surrounded they did not surrender for some time. The men, however, pressed gallantly forward and eventually got as far as Gallipoli Farm. The Germans here were very stout hearted and refused to surrender. One had a machine gun on top of a concrete dugout and, for some reason or other, perhaps excitement, the men could not bring him down. Following the brilliant example of one of the company commanders, the men eventually closed in and after a fierce hand to hand encounter, in which bomb and bayonet were freely used, the place fell.

On Hill 35 a 90 m.m. field gun of an old pattern manufactured by Krupps was captured, and altogether eight heavy and light machine guns fell into the hands of the Battalion. About forty prisoners were taken belonging chiefly to the 2nd Reserve Division of the Prussian Guards. The enemy machine guns were soon turned round and got into action against the Germans by those of the men who understood their use.

Towards 5-30 p.m. in the evening the enemy opened fire with a heavy barrage of all calibres. The fire was particularly intense at Gallipoli Farm, where the company commander had himself relieved the sentry on lookout at his headquarters, until he was blown almost senseless by the violence of the concussion of a shell which burst almost on top of him. Afterwards the Germans advanced, but they were seen by the men and repulsed by machine gun fire. A party of Germans was observed carrying a stretcher and a white flag. It was a favourite device of the enemy to pretend that they were carrying a stretcher when they were actually carrying a machine gun, and in consequence this particular party was soon dispersed.

Towards dark on the 21st the enemy put down another heavy barrage on the line of Somme Farm. He was apparently delivering another counter-attack. After it had been kept up some time great consternation prevailed at Battalion headquarters. No word had been received from the troops in front. Perhaps the enemy had captured the front positions, and that the line was lost. The barrage was still intense, and anyone who should dare to advance through it would expect to meet with almost certain death. Yet some one had to go to ascertain if all was well or ill. The Commanding Officer made arrangements to burn all papers and told everyone they must fight to the last where they stood. The Second in Command ultimately managed to get to Somme Farm and came back with the information that all was well, which was of inestimable worth, for had the British barrage lines been withdrawn, as had been suggested, the troops in front would all have been sacrificed.

On the 22nd September the Battalion was relieved. The greatest care was taken to get the captured machine guns that were not needed for the defence back to the transport lines. They were collected at Battalion headquarters and carefully escorted to the neighbourhood of the old British front line near Potijze, where they were met by the transport officer, and duly delivered to Divisional headquarters.

Having been relieved the men made their way back in small parties to Vlamertinghe, where the night was spent. The next day the Battalion moved by train to a camp by Watou. Two or three days were spent here, and then the Battalion detrained to go down south to join General Byng's Third Army.

LEMPIRE.

The train journey lasted all day and the Battalion detrained at Bapaume, and by a night march on a bright moonlight night marched to a Nissen hut camp between Barastre and Haplincourt, where it sojourned for a few days. During this time a few of the non-commissioned officers were able to visit the Somme battlefield, and locate a few of the graves of the men who had fallen a little over twelve months ago. A day's march on the 1st October brought the Battalion to Aizecourt-le-Bas, and after a night's rest it proceeded to St. Emilie, where the men were billeted amid the ruins of what had formerly been a sugar factory. During the march it was made plainly evident to all with what thoroughness the work of destruction had been carried out by the Germans. The villages were not merely in ruins. Every house and every room had been rendered useless as a billet or shelter of any kind. The cellars had been filled with stones or refuse, so that even these were of no use. The trees had all been wantonly destroyed. Even small fruit trees of only a few years' growth did not escape the axe. The wells had all been blown in, and in many cases they were poisoned as well. The churches were treated exactly the same as the houses. The whole region was desolate. There were no civilian inhabitants, and soldiers were the only occupants of this wilderness.

After a few days in the Sugar Factory the Battalion moved to the forward positions at Lempire. This sector was very different from any sector the Battalion had occupied. There was no trench system comprising front and support trenches. The front was held by means of isolated posts occupied by a platoon or a company as the case might be, and these posts were linked up by means of communication trenches, so that they could be visited. There being little artillery on either side, the whole sector was very quiet, and as the lines were far apart there was little sniping.

The Battalion did one tour in Cat, Fleeceall and Grafton Posts in front of Lempire, and then moved up to the Ossus sector. Though the Germans had destroyed all buildings behind the British line, the buildings behind the German lines were intact, and the men experienced the unpleasant sight of the comfortable chateaux and houses in which the German troops were billeted when they themselves were very badly off in this respect.

Three companies had been in the front in the Lempire position, and as three companies were necessary to take over the Ossus sector, one company had to do two successive tours. It was a poor relief to have to move from one portion of the front line to another, especially as this company had only one subaltern. The sector held by the Battalion was roughly 2,000 yards, and consequently the three front companies each had from six to seven hundred yards. The trench strength of the companies was somewhere between eighty and ninety, the numbers not having been made up after the Ypres casualties, and consequently there was a great amount of work for everyone to do.

On the 18th the Battalion moved to reserve at Vaughan's Bank by Epéhy, from whence on the 22nd it moved into reserve at Tincourt. The American Railway Engineers had constructed a light railway from Epéhy to Tincourt, and they expressed their readiness to convey the Battalion there by rail. Their offer was gladly accepted, and the Battalion duly arrived at the station and entrained. There was a slight incline to commence and the numbers that arrived exceeded the haulage capacity of the only serviceable locomotive at the station, and consequently no progress was made. As there was no telegraph a message had to be sent on foot for another engine, which came along after a long wait, and eventually a start was made. The couplings were bad and the train soon broke into three portions. As the way was downhill the various sections glided down to the next station independently. Here there was another train and a loop line, and it also happened that one train was too long for the loop. Nothing daunted, the railway engineers indulged in a considerable amount of shunting, and decided to take a portion of the waiting train back with the troop train. All went well until the next incline was reached. There was a great strain on the engine, but eventually after charging the hill three or four times, accompanied by much racing of engines and skidding of wheels, the top was reached, and the Battalion got to Tincourt having taken on the journey twice the time it would have taken to march the distance.

At Tincourt a pleasant week was spent, after which the Battalion returned to the Birdcage sector, the portion of which immediately in front of Eagle Quarry was the scene of much minenwerfer activity.

THE BATTLE OF CAMBRAI.

No particularly arduous duty was assigned to the Battalion in connection with the operations on the 20th November. To divert the attention of the enemy from other troops who were attacking the Knoll, a few hundred yards on the right, the Battalion was ordered to place a dummy tank and dummy men out in no man's land in front of the vicinity of the Birdcage, and shortly after zero these were put in operation by means of wires. Naturally the Battalion came in for a good deal of the retaliatory fire of the enemy, but few casualties took place. Incidentally the enemy claimed to have repulsed an attack on this front, from which it follows that the dummies had been efficacious.

The Germans had been driven back by the surprise attack of the British, and Cambrai was nearly reached. The fighting died down in a few days, but on the 30th Cavalry General von der Marwitz delivered his counter-attack. He selected not the apex of the salient that had been driven into the German line, but the portion of the line to the south of it, which was so weakly held. On the morning of the 30th the Battalion was in support to the 165th Brigade in some dugouts in Lempire.

A warning had been received during the course of the night that an enemy attack was imminent, and the order was given to "stand to" well before dawn. At "stand to" all was perfectly quiet. The expected attack had not developed. The men stood down and a normal day was anticipated. At breakfast time there sounded a heavy barrage a mile or two to the north, and afterwards shells began to fall in the village. Large gas shells were creating a cloud near by, and a rumour came that the Germans had broken through at the Birdcage. The troops had such confidence in the other battalions in the Brigade that the rumour was not believed. Later a message came from Headquarters that the line further north had broken. Lempire must be held at all costs, and the Battalion was ordered to dig a line running east and west on the high ground to the north of the village, so as to command the ground as far as Holt's Bank. This was then in the possession of the Germans, who were within a few hundred yards of Epéhy, and if this latter place had fallen the Battalion would have been in great danger of being surrounded. The men dug in under shell fire, and in full view of the enemy, while a large squadron of enemy aeroplanes circled overhead, and turned their machine guns on the men as they were digging. Fortunately few casualties were incurred. In the afternoon one company was sent to form a defensive flank at Priel Bank, and another to reinforce the 6th Liverpool Rifles at Cruciform Post. On the 2nd December the Battalion took over from the 6th Liverpools, and had the task of putting the line from Heythrop Post, Cruciform Post, to Priel Bank in a state of defence. These places were almost isolated during the day, and it was only at great risk that they could be visited. The post at Catelet Copse was almost a bait to the enemy, one of whom walked up to it. Even the Battalion headquarters at F.4. Central were under close rifle fire. In fact there were no troops in front of Headquarters, and it can be said that on this occasion the Battalion headquarters were in the front line.

On the 5th December the Battalion was relieved by a battalion from Brigadier-General Ramsay's 48th Brigade, and he visited his former command next morning at St. Emilie. Of the officers that had served under him in the 1st Division, only two then remained, and they were pleased to see their former commanding officer once more. That day the Battalion went by motor lorry to billets in Péronne, where four days were spent. A few civilians had returned to this ruined town, and had opened shops at which fish and vegetables could be bought. These civilians were much impressed by the nightly retreat sounded by the bugles and drums which had attained a high pitch of efficiency. A long tedious railway journey on the 10th brought the Battalion to Maroeuil. The night was spent in "Y" hutments, and it then entered General Horne's First Army.

It left Maroeuil on the 12th and marched to Bailleul-aux-Cornailles, a village it was to visit later in August, 1918. The next day Eps was reached, and on the following day the Battalion arrived at its destination at Lisbourg, where it was to remain until the end of January, which meant a six week's rest.

Here the men were billeted in the peasants' byres, which were in rather a dilapidated condition. The training was chiefly devoted to musketry. The bomb had gone out of fashion, and it was realised that the principal weapon of the infantryman was the rifle. According to the orders of the Divisional Commander each company built a thirty yards' range for itself, and a two hundred yards' range was allotted to the Battalion. Snow fell but that made no difference to the training programme. The men had to lie on the frozen snow to fire the various practices, and bearing in mind that the rifles were very cold to handle, the results attained were excellent.

Christmas was spent here, and the Christmas dinner which took place in the school and a large barn was a great success, and demonstrated the good feeling that existed between the officers and men. A few days afterwards the Battalion was visited by Lieutenant-Colonel Luther Watts, O.B.E., V.D., the Town Major of St. Pol, and who had commanded the Battalion prior to the war, and at Dunfermline and Tunbridge Wells. Those of the officers and men who had served under him in England were pleased to see their former commanding officer once more.

While at Lisbourg efforts were made to induce the men to invest in War Saving Certificates. At first they were somewhat reluctant, saying that they did not wish to hand back their pay which they had earned. Lectures on the subject were delivered to them, and when the scheme was fully explained, and they understood the necessity for money in order to carry on the war, they readily responded, and over £1,000 was subscribed by the officers and men, which was the highest figure attained in the Division. This was an achievement of which the Battalion was justly proud, and shows the keenness and interest the men displayed in their Regiment, and the cause for which they were fighting.

In consequence of the reduction of the number of infantry battalions in the organisation of the British division from twelve to nine, the "first ninth" being the junior battalion in the Brigade was split up. A selected party of the officers and men was detailed for the second line Battalion, and they were regarded with envy by the less fortunate. The remainder was split up into drafts for the 1st, 4th, and 12th King's. The day of the break up was a very sad one indeed. To a soldier his regiment is his home, and to be called upon to leave it, to sever his friendships and to lose his comrades of many a tragic day is for him very bitter. It is not untrue to say that as the drafts were leaving and comrades were saying "Goodbye," several of the soldiers, who had braved nearly inconceivable terrors, were almost in tears. As was feared at the time the "Goodbye" in many cases was for ever, as many were killed shortly afterwards by the German offensive in March. The Divisional Commander and several officers from other units came to say "Farewell" to the Battalion they were never to see again. A note of sadness is struck in the following order which was issued:—

55th (West Lancashire) Division,

Special Order of the Day.
31st January, 1918.

On the departure from the Division of three Battalions, the 1-8th The King's Liverpool Regt. (Liverpool Irish), 1-9th The King's Liverpool Regt., and 1-5th Loyal North Lancashire Regt., I wish to assure all officers, warrant officers, non-commissioned officers and men belonging to them, how greatly I, and I am sure, everyone in the Division, regrets their loss.

Some, I am glad to say, remain with us.

As to the battalions themselves, I refuse to regard the separation as permanent, and I look forward confidently to the day when they will rejoin their old Division.

They have had their full share in all the hard fighting of the past two years, and have helped to make and maintain the reputation which the Division has gained, a reputation which, I am sure, makes every member of it proud of belonging to it. As for myself, to have commanded it during these years is the highest privilege.

I hope that eventually the Liverpool Irish, the 9th King's, and the 5th Loyal North Lancs. may rejoin our ranks, and that the final blow may be given shoulder to shoulder with them.

Till they come back again I wish them, on the part of the Division and myself, all good fortune and success, and can assure them that we shall watch their career as keenly as if they were still with us.

H.S. JEUDWINE,
Major General,
Commanding 55th Division.

Unfortunately the hopes of the Major General were not realised. He never saw this Battalion on parade again.

CHAPTER IV.
THE 57TH DIVISION.

The second line Battalion was formed at Blackpool in 1914, and on the departure of the first Battalion from Tunbridge Wells for France its place was taken by the second Battalion. For a considerable time it carried out training at Tunbridge Wells, Ashford, Oxted, Maidstone, Canterbury and Blackdown, from which place it departed on the 17th February, 1917, for France.

It was commanded by Lieutenant-Colonel Leggatt, and formed part of Brigadier-General Paynter's 172nd Infantry Brigade of the 57th Division, which was a Division composed entirely of Lancashire troops, and a sister Division to the 55th.

After being delayed for three days at Folkestone, it crossed to Boulogne on the 20th. The next day it was moved by train to the neighbourhood of Bailleul, and from there by stages to the village of Erquinghem, south of Armentières. After a week spent in training, completing equipment, and reconnoitring the sector to be taken over, it went into the Bois Grenier sector. During the first tour in the trenches, the front held was twice extended and eventually it held a front of one and three-quarter miles. Here the Battalion remained for nearly seven months. The sector had been held by the New Zealanders, and was one of the quietest on the whole British front, but orders were now given to liven things up in order to keep as many enemy troops opposite the sector as possible, and distract their attention from the impending operations at Messines on the left. This object was achieved by considerable activity, patrols, and artillery bombardments. The extent of the front held entailed a good deal of exertion in the way of working parties, both to prevent the breast-works from falling into complete decay and to keep the trenches drained; and though the Battalion was very fortunate and suffered comparatively few casualties, the numbers steadily dwindled as no drafts were forthcoming. The enemy had very little artillery opposite this sector, and relied mainly for his defence on minenwerfers which he used liberally and skilfully, harassing the Battalion with an exceedingly heavy bombardment about once a fortnight.

In August, the Commanding Officer left the Regiment and the command was taken over by Lieutenant-Colonel Manger. The following month the Battalion was taken out of the line for a rest, and was billeted in the village of Febvin Palfart. Here it remained for a month reorganising and practising the attack, special attention being paid to the method of taking "pill boxes" by encirclement.

In October the "Second Ninth" set out for the Ypres salient, and on arriving at Proven was accommodated in tents. There it was told that the Division was about to take part in an attack on Passchendaele, but the weather conditions were so bad that, after an attack by one of the other brigades in the Division, the offensive was finally abandoned. The Battalion then held the shell crater line in front of Langemarck for a few days at the beginning of November, sustaining a considerable number of casualties. The Division was then withdrawn and the Battalion was put into rest billets at Nielles. After about a month spent there in re-organisation and training for the attack, it moved up to Emile Camp, just outside Elverdinghe. The weather was bitterly cold and the ground frozen hard. On Christmas Day the Battalion went into the shell crater line at Poelcappelle, and spent four days there. The weather conditions were very severe, snow had fallen, the ground was wet and the machine gun fire very active. The first week in January the Regiment was once again in its original sector at Armentières. Here things were comparatively quiet, though the trenches were in a very bad condition, and the danger of trench feet was considerable. The Battalion carried out a very successful raid on the 1st February. Several patrols had been sent out to locate the best place of entry into the enemy line. After an intense bombardment on the selected spot, a party was able to enter and secure a few prisoners. This was the most successful raid the Division had accomplished.

The remnants of the first Battalion left Lisbourg for Steenwerck, where they spent a few days awaiting the return of the second Battalion from the trenches. The two units met at Waterlands Camp outside Armentières, and were united to form one battalion. The union, though imperative, was distasteful to some, as many officers and non-commissioned officers had to relinquish acting ranks which they had held for some time, and it perhaps gave rise to some jealousy which fortunately disappeared in time.

After a few days spent at Waterlands, the Battalion moved into support at Erquinghem, with one company in the Lunatic Asylum at Armentières, and after a short stay it did one tour in the line near Houplines, and then went to Estaires, where it was in support to the Portuguese Army.

This was then a quiet country town in which the shops were still open, and incidentally doing a very good trade, and it had suffered little from the effects of artillery. During the next three months it was to be reduced to ruins. The Battalion was accommodated in a Nissen hut camp just outside the town, where the company commanders had an opportunity of completing the re-organisation of their companies.

On the 13th March the non-commissioned officers celebrated the anniversary of the Battalion's first arrival in France by arranging a kind of concert in one of the estaminets in Estaires. This was the last occasion before the Armistice on which such a celebration took place, and it has developed into an annual reunion of the senior non-commissioned officers.

Towards the end of the month the Battalion left Estaires for the Armentières front, and on the 21st March Ludendorff's advance commenced on the 5th Army front, at which time the Battalion was in line in the Fleurbaix sector. Ten days later the unit was relieved and marched to Estaires, where it arrived on the morning of the 1st April. Leaving this town later in the day, it made Haverskerque that night, left there the next day for Steenwerck, and entrained for Doullens. Detraining at Doullens at 1 a.m. on the 3rd, the Battalion proceeded by night march to Sus St. Leger. The night was dark and the roads were in bad condition and a few men fell out, but on the whole, the march discipline was good. On the 5th the Battalion moved to Warluzel, where it remained for three days and then proceeded to Thièvres, staying there four days. These moves meant a great strain on everyone. To march in full pack on bad roads with motor lorries splashing mud, day after day, is an ordeal. In each village a fresh start had to be made. Billets had to be found and allotted, fire orders put up and billet guards mounted. Latrines and cook-houses had to be improvised, and the usual foot inspections were made. Besides this the usual routine returns had to be rendered to people that sat in comfortable offices, and the men had to do ration fatigues and guards. Though the difficulties of the companies were great, the difficulties of the Quartermaster's department and that of the Transport Officer were much greater. The Quartermaster had not enough room to take the stores he wished, and the Transport Officer had as much as he could do to carry all the stores there were.

On the 12th a move was made to Sombrin, and the next day the Battalion left Sombrin late in the afternoon for an unknown destination. Even the Colonel did not know, and there was a vague rumour that the Brigade staff were to look after the unit. The men marched over bad roads and in the dark, and ultimately they were turned into a wood and told there were no billets, and they could bivouac for the night. Officers and men lay down on the damp earth where they were and slept. Fortunately it did not rain. A few tents came up very late, and in the darkness they could not be pitched, but they were spread out and thrown over the men as they lay sleeping on the ground. Fires could not be lighted as the enemy aeroplanes would have used them as aiming marks. In the morning the Battalion on awaking found it was just outside Pas, in what was called Beaucamp Ravine. Here it remained for two days, and then moved to Hénu, where the men pitched a camp in a field, and there the Battalion remained for a little over a fortnight. But it was no rest camp. The weather was very bad and the ground became wet and sodden. Every alternate day large working parties, which consumed almost all the available men, were detailed for work on the rear lines of defence, that were being hastily constructed, in view of the imminence of a fresh enemy offensive. On the intervening days training took place. There was a thirty yards' range in a ravine just in the rear of the camp, where some very interesting competitions took place. Rifle sections were pitted against Lewis gun sections and it was found that, in some platoons a rifle section of eight men was able to get as many shots on the target as the Lewis gun, and it was noticed incidentally that after two hundred rounds the Lewis gun became far too hot to handle. It was a much over-rated weapon, and was only effective in the hands of highly trained men.

Several reconnaissances were made by the officers while at Hénu. The forward area was visited again and again. Defence schemes were studied and prepared, but these tended to become a little too complex, and had it been necessary to put them into operation something would surely have gone wrong.

The morale at this time was low. The extent of the losses on the 5th and 2nd Army fronts were known. The enemy was using British 60-pounder guns against the area occupied by the Battalion, but as the enemy gunners did not thoroughly understand how to set the fuses, the shells were all blind. The Germans seemed to be able to advance whenever they wished, whereas the British had miserably failed at Ypres the last year. The men were not in very good fettle owing to the several recent marches, and the chance of complete victory seemed to be remote. Nevertheless there were many who kept cheerful and intended like game cocks to fight to the last.

The first week in May the Battalion went into line at Gommecourt. The other two units in the Brigade were in the outpost line, and the 9th King's was in close support in Gommecourt Park. It was accommodated in what were formerly the front line enemy positions in 1916. It was an education in military engineering to examine them. The trenches were deep and wide, and there were traverses every few yards. They were revetted with hurdles and planks of timber which were kept in position by iron pickets, which were securely wired to anchor pickets driven sideways into the walls of the trench. So well anchored were the revetments that in spite of the continuous bombardments of the Somme Battle they were still in position. The whole line was stellated with concrete machine-gun emplacements, which gave a perfect command over the former British front line trenches. Armoured look-out posts for sentries were at the top of all the dugout stairs. The dugouts were deeply mined and well timbered, and would provide shelter for a large garrison.

In front of the trenches was a dense wire entanglement at least twenty yards broad, and although it had suffered much from artillery fire it was still an obstacle which was only passable by infantry in certain places where lanes had been made. Anyone who saw this entanglement did not wonder why the British attack on the Somme on the 1st July, 1916, failed. Several graves of the fallen could be seen here and there in the wire.

It was very interesting to walk through the Park. Despite the bombardments it had undergone, the rides were clearly marked, and several trees were still alive, including one or two fine copper beeches. Wild hyacinths and other flowers were blooming in profusion, and a cuckoo, with doubtful wisdom, persisted in remaining in its usual haunts.

While in this position the whole Battalion was engaged in reclaiming old trenches, digging new ones, and putting the area in a position of defence and establishing a central keep.

On the 11th May the enemy shelled Foncquevillers, a village immediately in rear of the Battalion's position, with gas shells, most of which were charged with mustard gas, and some of the gas being inhaled by the men of the Battalion twenty-four casualties were sustained.

Three days later the Battalion took over the front line, the Headquarters still remaining at Gommecourt, but in another part of the village. The trenches were very wet, and reminded one of the Loos trenches in 1915. It was a time of great patrol activity. No one was quite sure where the Germans were and in what force. Daylight and night fighting patrols constantly left the British lines, and almost invariably came across parties of the enemy, but as the enemy was caged in by wire prisoners could not be obtained.

In this sector the enemy had full observation of the village from Rossignol Wood, and men from other units were in the habit of betraying the location of dumps and headquarters by walking along the roads in daylight instead of through the communication trenches. This enabled the enemy to note ways of approach which he could shell after nightfall, and so inflict casualties on working parties. To prevent this, two snipers were told off to lie in the grass and fire above the head of anyone who did not keep in the communication trenches. The scheme was efficacious; the men respected the snipers more than the enemy, and little trouble was given afterwards by the casual visitor to the sector.

One fine morning the enemy elected to shell Battalion headquarters, to the great amusement of the companies in the front line. Two out of the three mine entrances to the dugout occupied by the headquarter's personnel received direct hits and were blocked. The Second in Command then had the unpleasant duty of crawling out of the third entrance to see if all was well. Fortunately nothing untoward had taken place except three slight casualties.

On relief two companies went to the Chateau de la Haie, and the two other companies and Headquarters to Rossignol Farm, a large monastic farm of considerable age. There was an enormous byre partitioned off into several pig styes, and this was allotted to the officers, one pig stye for each officer. The War Diary for the next three weeks gives an interesting and accurate account of what took place, so the following extract is included:—

May 24th.—Battalion headquarters moved up to Chateau de la Haie, and Lieutenant-Colonel F.W.M. Drew, D.S.O., being in need of a rest, was evacuated sick, and Major S.C. Ball, M.C., assumed command. While at this Chateau, Battalion headquarters had the pleasure of being closely associated with the headquarters of the 1st Battalion Royal Munster Fusiliers; and it is interesting to record that this was not the first time that the Battalion had the honour of working in conjunction with this illustrious regiment. Many members of the Battalion could clearly remember how the 9th had the honour of relieving the 2nd Royal Munster Fusiliers, elements of which were incorporated in the 1st Royal Munster Fusiliers, after the Battle of Loos, in the 3rd Infantry Brigade of the 1st Division.

May 25th.—BEER TRENCH.—The Battalion relieved the 1st Battalion Royal Munster Fusiliers in Beer Trench, where "A" and "D" Companies and the Lewis gunners of "B" were accommodated. "B" and "C" Companies remained in the Chateau de la Haie Switch. There was heavy shelling in "A" Company's area during the evening, but no casualties were sustained. The Battalion came tactically under the orders of the 170th Infantry Brigade while in Beer Trench.

May 26th.—Gas shells known as yellow cross shells, were fired over "A" Company's sector in the early morning. The men quickly adjusted their masks, and no casualties were sustained. The rest of the day passed quietly.

May 27th to 29th.—These days were fairly quiet.

May 29th.—RUM TRENCH.—The Battalion relieved the 2-4th Loyal North Lancashire Regiment and occupied the reserve position in the Left Brigade Sector. "B" Company and Headquarters were in Gommecourt Wood. "A" Company was in the centre with posts in Gommecourt Trench, and "C" Company was on the left flank in Pigeon Wood. "D" Company was in reserve with orders to man a strong point, known as Julius Point, in case of an attack. Opportunity was afforded of studying the solidarity of the enemy forms of revetment, their fortified sentry boxes, observation posts, and the thoroughness of the mined dugouts, several of which were occupied by the Battalion.

May 30th—31st.—These days were spent in comparative quietness, and the Battalion furnished several working parties. There was abnormal sickness during this tour in the trenches, due in all probability to the effects of gas.

June 1st.—GOMMECOURT.—The Battalion was in reserve to the Brigade in the Left Brigade Sector at Gommecourt with Headquarters in the old German support line, north of Gommecourt Wood, which was renamed Rum Support. The companies were disposed from right to left in order, "B," "A" and "C" in Gommecourt Trench and Gommecourt Support. "D" Company was in reserve. The companies were housed in mined dugouts made by the enemy, and again evidence of the industry of the Germans was seen in the mined dugouts, armoured sentry boxes, substantial revetments and belts of wire entanglements.

At morning "stand to," the enemy put down a barrage on the Divisional Front. The S.O.S. went up in several places and our artillery—some of which was immediately in rear—opened with rapid fire. It transpired later that the enemy raided the Right Brigade sector without success. The usual working parties were provided in the evening.

June 2nd.—The IV. Corps Commander visited the Battalion's sector. The Battalion did considerable work in its own sector digging rifle slits, and making baby elephant dugouts, besides providing the Royal Engineers with the usual working parties.

June 3rd.—The day passed in comparative tranquillity. Owing to the good weather prevailing at this period our observers were able to observe well behind the enemy lines. Occasionally they could see small bodies of the enemy moving about and sometimes horses grazing.

June 4th.—The day was spent very quietly, and there is nothing of interest to record.

June 5th.—The Brigadier commanding 172nd Infantry Brigade visited the Battalion and expressed his appreciation of the wiring done at Salmon Trench. Visibility was very good in the evening, and several parties of Germans were again seen.

June 6th.—The enemy opened a harassing fire on Battalion headquarters with 77 m.m. guns and 10.5 c.m. howitzers, firing with occasional short intervals until 3 p.m.

June 7th.—The day was spent very quietly and there is nothing of interest to relate.

June 7th—8th.—The Battalion relieved the 2-4th Battalion South Lancashire Regiment in the left section of the Left Brigade Front. Companies were disposed as follows:—Left front company, "A." Centre company, "D." Right front company, "C." Reserve company, "B." Battalion headquarters were established in Salmon Trench in the vicinity of a locality known as Salmon Point.

June 9th.—IN THE LINE.—The enemy displayed more than usual activity. The Brigadier General visited the sector.

June 10th.—Some rain fell during the day. The enemy displayed his usual artillery activity. Two enemy aeroplanes, one of which was a Halberstadter, flew over the Battalion area at a low altitude for some time.

June 11th.—The day was fairly quiet, our forward posts in front of Rossignol Wood were troubled by our own artillery which persistently fired short.

June 12th.—The enemy was noticeably quieter.

June 13th.—The Duke of Marlborough and Mr. Winston Churchill visited the Battalion sector, accompanied by the Divisional Commander.

June 14th.—Artillery activity at night has quietened considerably. Our gunners still continued to harass the enemy with an occasional *rafale* from their field guns.

The Battalion found a wiring party to assist the 2-4th Battalion South Lancashire Regiment to wire Biez Wood. The Brigadier General visited the sector.

June 14th—15th.—The Battalion was relieved by the 2-6th Battalion Liverpool Regiment. During the relief the enemy artillery was very active.

June 15th.—ROSSIGNOL FARM.—On relief the Battalion was disposed as follows:—"A" and "D" Companies at Chateau de la Haie; "B" and "C" Companies and Battalion headquarters at Rossignol Farm.

In May and June the Gommecourt sector was active, and the artillery fire on both sides was severe. The enemy employed a shell with an instantaneous fuse called the E.K.Z. fuse, which functioned before the shell buried itself and so gave the shell a very great splinter effect. It was usual for the enemy to fire on cross roads and similar targets in salvoes of four. The British artillery replied and kept up a lively fire most of the time, and it appeared to have the ascendency. Gas shells were frequently used on both sides.

Early in July the Battalion came out to rest at Authie, where it was accommodated under canvas. Here it was that Lieutenant-Colonel Lord

Henry Seymour, D.S.O., of the Grenadier Guards, took command. Training for the attack took place in some cornfields near to the camp, and particular attention was paid to the keeping of direction in the advance, the tactical employment of Lewis guns and the envelopment of machine gun nests. The fighting had become more open this year than it had been in 1917, and consequently the men had to be kept up to date. To consolidate a position the men were taught to form platoon strong points with the flanks refused or bent back so as to be able to meet an attack from any direction. Unfortunately the corn crops were spoilt by the training of the troops.

While at Authie, sports took place, and in the Brigade sports the Battalion secured seven first, eight second, and one third prize. The Army Rifle Competitions took place here, and No. 6 platoon of "B" Company won the eliminating competition in the Brigade, but unfortunately failed to win the Divisional competition.

Then followed a period of meanderings which lasted for a month, and which at the time were difficult to understand. On the 29th July the Battalion left Authie and marched to billets at Warluzel by the following route: Pas, Grincourt, and Couterelle. The march was rather severe as the weather was very hot, and it needed the greatest firmness on the part of the officers to prevent the men from falling out. The next day the Battalion paraded at 6-15 a.m., and marched to Agnez-les-Duisans *via* Hermaville, where it arrived in the afternoon.

In the evening of the following day the Battalion paraded and marched to Arras, entering the city by the Baudimont Gate, and the men were billeted for the night in the Spanish houses in the Grande Place. In the evening of the next day the Battalion paraded in the Square and marched to Wakefield Camp by Roclincourt. While in Arras the troops found an old hat shop and great amusement was caused by the soldiers arraying themselves in ladies' hats, which gave them a very strange appearance. A tall silk hat very much out of fashion was reserved for the officers, which they tried on in turn.

A week or so was spent in training at Roclincourt, and on the 9th the Battalion took over the outpost zone in the Gavrelle-Fampoux sector. The companies were taken up to the forward area by a light railway, and this was the only occasion on which the Battalion was taken to the forward area in such a manner.

The positions occupied gave a good view over the enemy hinterland. From the Battalion headquarters at the Point du Jour, factory chimneys could be seen smoking in several villages behind the German line, and the clock on Douai Church was clearly visible. Occasionally a train was seen moving, and now and then a party of Germans was observed. Behind the British line lay the rolling Artois country which was fundamentally agricultural, and in front there loomed in the distance an industrial manufacturing district, which seemed a far-off civilization in contrast to the devastation behind. It was a time of great aeriel activity on both sides. Battles were fought at high altitudes, of which one was scarcely conscious except when one of the combatant machines fell headlong to earth. As a means of self protection Lewis guns were placed on aeriel mountings, and a sharp look out was kept for any daring Halberstadter that should venture too low. The weather at the time was fine, and the tour was regarded as one of the easiest the men had been called upon to do.

On the 17th August the Battalion was relieved just before midnight, and marched to Anzin, where it arrived at 4-30 a.m. the next morning, and the men had breakfast. Later it entrained for Bailleul-aux-Cornailles, where four days were spent. On the 21st an order was received about 10 p.m., (after the men had bedded down) to move at once. The move was quite unexpected as everyone believed the Battalion was to stay in the village for several days longer. Kits were hastily packed in the darkness, and in an hour the Battalion was ready to move. Fosseux was reached in the early morning, breakfast taken, and the men rested until 1 p.m. In the evening another sudden message ordered a night march to Boucquemaison, which was reached early on the 23rd, and the men rested during the day time, paraded at nightfall and marched to Barly.

These marches were perhaps rather fatiguing, but as they took place at night and the weather was very pleasant, they were not as bad as they might have been. The march discipline was excellent and scarcely any men fell out. The companies as day was breaking presented nevertheless a worn-out appearance. The men were dusty and tired out as they trudged in the mist of the morning, with the field kitchen and Lewis gun cart in the rear. The cooks were doing their best to get the fire lighted to boil the water for breakfast. The pack animals seemed to wonder what necessity there could be for all this marching, and the company charger, generally a very dejected jade, feeling as proud of his position as his mean station in the equine world would permit, persistently refused to keep his proper position when a halt was called.

It was during the march to Barly that the men were told, during a halt at midnight, that victory was certain, and that Marshal Foch had ordered everyone to advance. This news instantly raised the *morale* of every one, and the rest of the journey seemed more pleasant than usual.

THE SECOND BATTLE OF ARRAS.

A day's halt took place at Barly, where the surplus personnel was left while the fighting men left for Bellacourt. The next day the Battalion left and, passing *en route* Ficheux and Blaireville, the villages in front of which it had spent so many weary months in 1916, arrived at Mercatel.

On the 27th August the Battalion proceeded, dressed in fighting order, to the Hindenburg Line, *via* Henin, and took over trenches in V. 7.c. On the 28th a warning order was received at 6 a.m. that the Battalion would attack that day. Operation orders followed later. The two leading companies were to assemble at Humber Redoubt and Mole Lane, and the other two companies in the rear. The first objective assigned to the Battalion was Hoop Lane and the second the village of Riencourt. Flanks were given and zero was fixed for 12-30 p.m.

It was fortunate that a warning order had been given as otherwise the companies would not have been in position in time. At 12-30 p.m. the barrage came down and the men commenced to move forward. The going at first was not easy, owing to the wire and numerous shell holes. Shortly after zero the contact aeroplane unfortunately received a direct hit by a shell and crashed to earth. Very heavy machine gun fire was directed against the leading companies from Copse Trench, which brought about many casualties. Fag Alley was reached and in its vicinity several machine guns were captured, and the teams either killed or taken prisoners. From this point to the first objective the resistance was not so strong, and on reaching it red flares were lit.

About 1-50 p.m. the Battalion continued the advance from the first objective, and swung left in the direction of the village of Hendicourt. The resistance became stronger. The enemy was using his machine guns boldly. Some of these were outflanked and captured with a few light minenwerfers. About fifty prisoners, chiefly belonging to the 121st and the 180th Infantry Regiments of the 26th Reserve Division were taken, along with a few Uhlans. Eventually the fringe of Hendicourt was reached, and several men entered the village. As it was reported that there were no British troops on either side of the village it was decided on the spot to withdraw to Cemetery Avenue temporarily. "D" Company was endeavouring to get round the north side of the village but was held up by heavy machine gun fire from Crow's Nest. Owing to this machine gun fire and to the fact that the left flank of the Battalion was in the air, and that the British artillery was shelling the village, it was decided to consolidate Cemetery Trench. Meanwhile some enemy field gunners were firing at the British at very close range. By this time the troops had got very mixed up, and it was essential that the commanders on the spot should organise what men they found near by. This was done and the Battalion remained in its consolidated positions until the next day, when at noon it was withdrawn to Copse Trench and afterwards to a bivouac area at Henin.

Unfortunately, Lord Henry Seymour was wounded on the 28th August and the command then devolved upon Major Ball. There was a great deal of re-organisation to be done. The surplus personnel rejoined. Lists of casualties had to be prepared, ammunition, flares, Verey lights, and iron rations had to be given out. New platoon rolls had to be made at once. Lost Lewis guns and spare parts had to be made up, as well as possible. As a temporary measure "A" and "C" Companies, now sadly depleted in numbers, were united to form "X" Company, while "B" and "D" Companies formed "Y" Company. This scheme was adopted so that the original companies and platoons would not sink their identities in that of a sister company. This re-organisation was completed, equipment made up, and all necessary stores given out within twenty-four hours, and the Battalion was again ready for action. The bivouac area was vacated at 4 p.m. on the 1st September, and the Battalion went to the Hindenburg Line, where a few hours were spent. It left the Hindenburg Line about 10-30 p.m. for Hendicourt. An unfortunate circumstance, however, had taken place. The intelligence section, which was to act as guides to take the companies to Hendicourt, was annihilated by a shell, and as a consequence it was very difficult to get there to time in view of the lack of guides. The Battalion was piloted by the Adjutant over numerous broken-in trenches, while enemy aeroplanes were disseminating bombs quite liberally.

Hendicourt was reached fifteen minutes before zero, which was at 5 a.m. One company was then ordered to advance in the direction of Riencourt, the fringe of which village it reached by advancing over the open under cover of the barrage and, incidentally, encountering the German barrage.

On this day the famous Drocourt-Quéant Switch, the last and perhaps the strongest line of resistance of the enemy, was completely broken. Months had been spent on its preparation and in making concrete machine gun emplacements and belts of barbed wire, and its fall in one day was remarkable.

Later in the day the companies went forward over the ground captured by the other units in the Brigade, and one or two patrols were sent out. The following evening the Battalion was withdrawn to a bivouac area outside Croisilles, which vicinity was shelled by a 350 m.m. Krupp gun. The Battalion was reorganised on a four-company basis once more the next day.

On the 7th September the Battalion proceeded, *via* Hendicourt and Riencourt, to a reserve position by Cagnicourt, and on the 10th the Battalion furnished two companies for manning the Buissy Switch in the rear of Inchy-en-Artois. Battalion headquarters were situated in the Hindenburg Line and the two forward companies were just on the fringe of Inchy, and accommodated in what had lately been the headquarters of the

115th Feldartillerie Regiment. The dugout was cut into the side of the road and consisted of several well-timbered rooms and there were about four entrances. This dugout was so well fitted that it actually contained a pump, to ensure an adequate supply of water for the garrison.

On the 11th September there was an attack by other units in the 57th Division in conjunction with the Guards Division on the east side of Inchy and Moeuvres, so as to secure the line of the Canal du Nord. The attack was covered by an intense bombardment of the enemy front positions and Bourlon Wood, and the advance of the infantry was covered by smoke. Officers from the Battalion observed the attack from Buissy Switch to note where lay the enemy barrage lines. The attack at Inchy was, unfortunately, a failure.

On the 12th the Battalion took over the defence of Inchy. The right company was located in Grabburg Post, and the left in a shell crater position by the Agache Springs. The other two companies were in support. The conditions were bad, and the men in front had to lie in their shell craters all day. As these generally contained water, the men got very wet. The village was incessantly shelled and periodically drenched with gas. Even night brought no respite and the guns still disgorged their fatal missiles. Some idea of the intensity of the shell fire may be gained from the following incident.

"A" Company headquarters and one platoon were quartered in a long cellar belonging to a factory. The cellar was divided into two compartments, and of these only the one further from the entrance was occupied. While the shelling was taking place the Company Commander was out interviewing the Commanding Officer and, returning to his headquarters, he saw shell after shell burst in the vicinity. When the intensity of the fire was somewhat mitigated, he returned to company headquarters and there saw a shell had entered and burst in the empty compartment. When he asked the men about it they did not know what had happened, and they even had not noticed it amid the several other shells that had burst close by.

While at Inchy the Battalion had the misfortune to lose its most popular officer, who was killed while doing a daylight patrol in Pavilland Wood. He had fought in the first Battle of Ypres in 1914 and had remained in France until wounded in 1917. Though blind in one eye and deaf in one ear, he insisted on returning to the battlefield after his wounds had healed. His conduct stands out in sharp contrast to the thousands who were evading service at home.

On the 16th September, the Battalion was relieved and marched by companies to a bivouac area by Bullecourt. On arrival a thunderstorm took place. The men were soon wet, the ground sodden, and the bivouac sheets caked with mud. To this was added the fact that fires and lights were not permitted on account of the enemy aeroplanes. The next day, however, was fine and everyone quickly dried. Of the village scarcely a vestige remained. Here and there the foundation of a wall was discernible in the mud. French villages are usually well wooded, but of all the trees in Bullecourt there was only one standing, and that had died from the effects of shell fire. The Battalion marched off next day and entrained by Boyelles, and after a short journey detrained at Beaumetz. Here the men saw once again the village they knew so well in 1916. It seemed strange that trains were running in the station now.

At Beaumetz the Battalion marched past some of its former billets to Bailleulment. Here a few days were spent in resting and training, and on the 25th September the Battalion marched to Beaumetz and by train and route march proceeded to a bivouac area at Lagnicourt.

On the 27th September the Battalion took part in the advance. The men got to the position of assembly in the Hindenburg Line and then passed through Moeuvres, crossed the Canal du Nord and advanced in artillery formation towards the southern corner of Bourlon Wood.

While coming over the crest just north of Anneux "A" Company came under the direct fire of a 105 m.m. enemy gun, the detachment of which was firing over open sights, and several casualties were sustained. The Battalion was soon held up by machine gun fire, but it afterwards advanced and took up a position between Anneux and Bourlon Wood. The 29th was spent in re-organisation.

On the 30th the Battalion paraded, and an attempt was made to carry on the attack. Unfortunately, the suburb of Proville had not been captured, as had been originally supposed, and the attack could not proceed on account of the heavy machine gun fire from the houses.

The Battalion was then withdrawn to La Folie Wood, where a few days were spent in old German shelters. The enemy evidently knew that the wood was occupied, for he persistently shelled it with his heavy batteries, and the trees served to intensify the sound of the explosions. Several 18-pounder guns and a battery of 8-inch howitzers were about a hundred yards or so in rear of the Battalion's position; and when an attack by one of the other units in the Division was in progress the noise was intense.

On the 5th October the Battalion took over the outpost zone at Proville, with headquarters at La Marlière. At this time there were few troops on the bridgehead east of the Canal de l'Escaut. The area was periodically searched by the enemy heavy artillery, and the posts at Proville suffered considerably from minenwerfer fire. On relief the Battalion returned to La Folie Wood.

When Cambrai fell on the 9th October the Battalion left for the Cantaing area and on the 11th moved to a bivouac area by Inchy. The next day it marched to Hermies, and there entrained for Bethune, where it arrived next day and marched to Douvrin.

It was now almost three years since the Battalion had been in the vicinity of Bethune, but there were still some present who could remember how the Battalion in the spring of 1915 had marched for the first time to the trenches in front of this town. The next day the Battalion went by motor lorries through Locon and other places the men had known so well in 1915 and, debussing near Laventie, the Battalion marched via Fromelles to Le Maisnil en Weppes. Passing through what was formerly no man's land at Laventie, the men were able to recognise the places they had held in the trenches in the early part of the year.

LILLE.

Three days were spent at Le Maisnil, during which the seizure of Lille was carefully studied by the officers and orders were given as to the mode of procedure should the enemy evacuate the town. On the 17th October at 1-15 p.m. the Battalion paraded in fighting order and advanced to the deliverance of the city. There was at this time a vague report that the enemy had departed, but it was not known to what point the British troops had then attained. There might have been troops between the Battalion and the enemy, and there might not. Road mines and "booby" traps were to be expected. The Battalion arrived at Haubourdin at 4 p.m., where there was a halt for a meal. On reaching the suburbs of Lille advance guards had to be sent out, as any point of vantage might have concealed an enemy machine gun. The canal on the west of the city was reached about 5 o'clock. The bridges had all been blown up, but the Pont de Canteleu, though broken in two and half in the canal, afforded a means of crossing one at a time.

At this bridge the greatest excitement prevailed. Crowds of women were singing the "Marseillaise." They surrounded the troops and could not be prevented from kissing the soldiers. So great was the crowd that the passage of the troops was impeded. Eventually the companies reached their allotted stations and formed guards on the various gates to prevent all egress. In this way the Battalion was the first infantry to reach the city. Actually the first to enter was "D" Company.

Here was a city without civil administration. The late authorities had been the Germans, and they had gone. There were no police and no post; the streets were unlit and the trams had long since ceased to run; garbage was deposited in the street and there putrified. There was a great shortage of food. The shops were empty, hundreds had died of want, and the strength of the inhabitants was very low.

For three days the Battalion remained on guard at the gates to prevent all egress of the inhabitants, as there were some residents in the city that the French authorities wished to arrest, and so it was necessary to prevent their escape before the French police arrived. Out of the men not actually on duty, a guard of honour was found to accompany M. Clemenceau on his triumphal entry into the city on behalf of the French Republic. It was an inspiring occasion, and the greatest enthusiasm prevailed. The Battalion on the 21st marched through Lille, being met by "A" Company at the Porte des Postes, to Ascq, where it stayed the night. The next day it moved to Willems on the Belgian frontier.

TOURNAI.

On the 24th October the Battalion took over the outpost zone at Froyennes by Tournai. This was a new kind of warfare. There were no trenches, no enemy line and no clearly defined British line. Sentry groups were located in houses, behind hedges and perhaps in a ditch on the side of the road. Sentries kept a look-out from a skylight window or gap in the hedge. Civilians were living in the same houses as the troops and some of these appeared rather friendly towards the enemy. One woman actually wished to take some washing to the Germans in Tournai. For the most part these civilians were women, and the soldiers admired their wonderful courage. Even though they were in the centre of the fighting they did not lose heart and there was no panic.

In the right company area was situated a chateau which had formerly been the headquarters of General von Quast, the commander of the Sixth German Army. Company headquarters were in the next chateau, the Chateau de Froyennes, belonging to the Germiny family, and the then occupier, Mademoiselle Thérèse de Germiny, who had remained, lent her boat to the Company, and several men were able to row on the ornamental lake which was situated at the side of the chateau in a beautiful park. One platoon was quartered in a restaurant which had a beautiful and rustic garden, though it was too near the enemy for the men to really enjoy the comfort it afforded. Another platoon found in a laundry a number of clean white shirts which the men readily donned.

Though the Germans had been defeated, they still continued to indulge in a lavish expenditure of ammunition. Probably they were firing so as to use up their remaining shells before evacuating. Day after day the park belonging to the Froyennes Chateau was searched by all manner of shell. So intense was the fire that it reminded one of the terrible moments of the Somme Battle. The Hospital or Convent in which one of the companies was located was subjected to incessant minenwerfer fire.

It is interesting to record that "A" Company elected to do the full tour of four days in the front position with the intention of spending all the next tour in support, an eventuality which did not take place as the Armistice intervened.

Coming out from Froyennes the Battalion was shelled on the road. Little did anyone think that night that the Battalion had finished with shell fire. For the men the war was over. Their last time in action was passed. Among those that trudged wearily out of action that night were a few who had landed at Le Havre with the Regiment more than three and a half years before. Though they did not realise it until much later these men were the lucky ones who were to survive the war.

The Battalion marched to Cornet and the next day to Hellemmes, outside Lille, for a period of rest. Here the men were quartered in a cotton spinning factory, the machinery of which was all utterly destroyed, and every man had his own bunk. The officers were billeted in private houses in the vicinity. While on parade on the morning of the 11th November it was announced to the men that the Armistice had been signed. The news of the cessation of hostilities was received by the soldiers without any manifestation of the joy or excitement that marked the occasion at home. The parade continued and the rest of the day was spent quite as usual. The news for which the men had waited so long seemed when it came to be almost too good to be true.

Some there were—savages by nature—who were not altogether glad. They had been taught to kill, and they wanted to kill. They thought the Germans had not been punished enough for their crimes and atrocities, and that the enemy country ought to suffer the same devastation as France. In the main, however, the men were glad that the war was virtually over. They would soon be able to return to their homes and live with their loved ones again. On the night of the 13th the reality of the terms of the Armistice was evidenced by the returning British prisoners of war from the German lines. A picquet was posted on the main road outside Battalion headquarters, and on arrival returning prisoners were escorted to a billet which was prepared for them. Fires were burning in the billet, and all of the late prisoners were supplied with a bed. A hot meal, tea and a rum ration were served to them as they arrived. By midnight about eighty had come through. The majority of them arrived in an exhausted condition, having marched between forty and fifty kilometres. Many were the stirring and pitiful stories recounted by these unfortunate fellows of the harsh treatment which they had received during their period of captivity. The ensuing days of the month were spent at Hellemmes under the command of Lieutenant-Colonel Dawson for a few days, and afterwards Lieutenant-Colonel M.E. Makgill-Crichton Maitland, D.S.O., of the Grenadier Guards, took command.

Training as usual was continued as it was not realised at the time that the fighting was finished. The parades took place in the vicinity of Fort Macmahon, which had been used by the Germans as quarters for prisoners of war. The conditions inside the fort were terrible and constituted strong evidence of the sufferings the prisoners of war must have endured. In view of the imminence of demobilisation, education classes were started, and much good work was done in this direction. In the evenings concerts and parties took place, and friendships soon sprang up between the soldiers and the Lilloises.

ARRAS.

It was soon decided that the Army was to be used for salvage work on the devastated area, and accordingly orders came for a move to the Arras area. On the 3rd December the Battalion left Lille, and after a march of roughly 15 miles it reached Carvin and spent the night in some German ammunition huts in a wood. The next day the Battalion passed through Lens, and one was surprised to see how near the Highlanders must have got to the town at the Battle of Loos. After leaving Lens the Battalion marched right through the centre of the district in which the Vimy Ridge Battles had taken place. The whole region was now desolate and deserted. After a march of twenty-one miles three of the companies marched to their billets at Etrun without the loss of a single man. This was a striking example of the efficiency of the Battalion and the standard of its march discipline.

A few days were spent in billets at Etrun and then the Battalion moved to a Nissen hut camp a short distance away at Maroeuil. Twelve months ago the Battalion had spent a night at the camp on its way to Lisbourg. The camp had been empty for some months and was in a bad condition, so that a great deal had to be done to make the huts habitable. Beds and tables had to be constructed, cook houses established and ovens built. Duckboard tracks had to be laid as the ground was muddy. In this work the men were assisted by some German prisoners who worked very well and thoroughly. No enmity was evinced by the men, who would give the prisoners food if not watched. So soon had the British soldiers forgotten their hatred of the Germans. The Battalion was given a large area to clear and every day large parties were engaged on salvage work. The afternoons were devoted to games and some very keen football matches took place.

Christmas time was an occasion for great rejoicing. A competition for the best decorated dining hut was held. Materials were not easily available and the ingenuity of the officers was taxed to the utmost. One company commander had a scenic artist among his men and he managed to secure an ample supply of paint. Others telegraphed to England for table decorations and some things could be bought in Arras. One sergeant-major borrowed bed sheets from some lady friend and these served as table cloths. The dining huts were consequently well decorated and comfortable, and eventually "B" Company secured the prize. Christmas Day was one of feasting. A cross country run the next day, in which all from Commanding Officer downward, took part wore off any evil effect.

Early in January a "Colour Party" left for Liverpool, where it received the colours of the Regiment from the Lord Mayor on the 7th January, and later brought them to the Battalion.

Demobilisation commenced in January, and by the end of February the disintegration of the Battalion was proceeding rapidly. The numbers dwindled so steadily that at length parades ceased. Men who had served and lived together for so long were parting and might perhaps never see each other again. Friendships of months' standing were now to come to an end. No bugle would ever call these men together again. They were each to return to their civilian life once more, and there seek their several fortunes.

The members of the Battalion took different paths. A large contingent ultimately made its way to Egypt as part of the garrison there. Others, members of the cadre, came home with the Colours in June and were received with due honour by the Lord Mayor. One or two isolated members crept up to the Rhine Army, where they had the pleasure of seeing the result of their comrades' work, and the Germans dejected and defeated. It was indeed gratifying to see British soldiers quartered in Bonn University, that home of "kultur" where the late Kaiser Wilhelm was educated. A reunion took place in St. George's Hall on the 30th May, 1919. Afterwards the Battalion ceased to exist as infantry, as the War Office changed it to a Battalion of Royal Engineers called the 2nd Battalion West Lancashire Divisional Royal Engineers, to which several of the officers transferred.

The work of the Battalion is done. By the bravery and industry of the officers and men, by the soldierly spirit with which all were imbued, by the discipline and good comradeship which kept all together working in harmonious union, the Battalion earned for itself a high reputation for efficiency in every direction. The work it was given to do has been done in a cheerful and thorough manner, and let there be inscribed, with due honour, upon the list of the illustrious regiments which have deserved well of their country, the name of the 9th Battalion of The King's (Liverpool Regiment) Territorial Force.

APPENDIX.

List of Decorations earned by officers and men while serving with the Battalion.

A BAR TO THE DISTINGUISHED SERVICE ORDER.

Lieutenant-Colonel LORD H.C. SEYMOUR.

THE DISTINGUISHED SERVICE ORDER AND THE MILITARY CROSS.

Captain R.C. WILDE.

THE DISTINGUISHED SERVICE ORDER.

Major-General F.W. RAMSAY
Lieutenant-Colonel H.K.S. WOODHOUSE
Lieutenant-Colonel F.W.M. DREW
Major F.S. EVANS
Major J. MAHONY, R.A.M.C.

THE MILITARY CROSS AND A BAR.

Captain E.H.G. ROBERTS
Captain C.G.R. HILL
Lieutenant S.H. RANDALL
Lieutenant A.O. WARDE

THE MILITARY CROSS.

Major J.W.B. HUNT
Major P.G.A. LEDERER
Captain S.T.J. PERRY
Captain E.L. MACKENZIE, R.A.M.C.
Captain W. RAINE
Captain A.G. WARDE
Captain E. PAYNE
Captain L.L.S. RICHER
Captain L.S. ELTON
Captain F. ATKINSON
Captain G.F. BUCKLE
Captain C.B. JOHNSON
Lieutenant R. DARLING
Lieutenant G.E. MORTON
Lieutenant A.C. SHEPHERD
Lieutenant F.E. BOUNDY

Lieutenant R.C.H. Ellam
Lieutenant A.M. Adams
Lieutenant W.L. Gelderd
Lieutenant W.G. Harrison, R.A.M.C.
Lieutenant W.J. Lunnon
Lieutenant L.T. Locan
Lieutenant A. Roe
Lieutenant W. Davenport
Lieutenant A.T. Barker
Lieutenant C. Stent
Lieutenant E.H. Maxwell
Regimental Sergeant-Major F.W. Miller
Regimental Sergeant-Major D. Roberts
Company Sgt.-Major F.E. Ash

THE DISTINGUISHED CONDUCT MEDAL, MILITARY MEDAL AND A BAR.

Sergeant W. Griffiths.

THE DISTINGUISHED CONDUCT MEDAL AND THE MILITARY MEDAL.

Company Sergeant-Major J. McCarten
Sergeant H. Williams
Sergeant H. Chisnall
Sergeant J.S. Morgan

THE DISTINGUISHED CONDUCT MEDAL.

Company Sergeant-Major P. Byrne
Company Sergeant-Major J. Owens
Company Sergeant-Major T. Brammer
Sergeant R. Williams
Sergeant A. Bennet
Sergeant J. Midghall
Lance-Sergeant J.W. Heap
Private W. Smith
Private F. Fowler

THE MILITARY MEDAL AND A BAR.

Sergeant R.D. Walker
Sergeant L.L. Delmas
Sergeant L. Bentley (D.C.M. with 4th Kings)

THE MILITARY MEDAL.

Company Sgt.-Major MEADOWS
Sergeant GILMARTIN
Sergeant P.J. HALL
Sergeant E. JONES
Sergeant MCCARTHY
Sergeant SHAW
Sergeant W.T. POPE
Sergeant R. LEE
Sergeant C. MADDEN
Sergeant STAPLETON
Sergeant MCNIFFE
Sergeant T. BALL
Lance-Sergeant PENNINGTON
Lance-Sergeant B. MADDEN
Lance-Sergeant W. MAWER
Corporal WINROW
Corporal E. HYLAND
Corporal H. READ
Corporal W. GRIFFIN
Corporal BROWN, R.A.M.C.
Corporal J. CLARKE
Corporal LEATHER
Corporal L. JONES
Corporal J. CORLESS
Corporal A. SALMON
Corporal W.H. COCKAYNE
Corporal J.R. SERVICE
Lance-Corporal A. HILTON
Lance-Corporal H. COOPER
Lance-Corporal H. JOHNSTONE
Lance-Corporal A. OTTY
Lance-Corporal SHIELDS
Lance-Corporal MARCHBANK
Lance-Corporal LEWIS
Lance-Corporal WESTWOOD
Lance-Corporal RAINFORD
Lance-Corporal H. MONTGOMERIE
Lance-Corporal T. GILL
Lance-Corporal J. TAYLOR
Lance-Corporal W. SALMON
Private W. WILLIAMS
Private A. TURNBULL

Private W. Hankey
Private R. Napier
Private W. Tyldesley
Private W.W. Oswald
Private T.W. Meers
Private T.V. Anderson
Private T. Buxton
Private J. Dilworth
Private J. Hanna
Private W. Hopley
Private T. Lloyd
Private W. Bleasdale
Private Foulkes
Private Morris
Private Shallcross
Private Entwistle
Private McDonald
Private Walker
Private Brough
Private E.O. Parry
Private Mottram
Private T. Hughes
Private H. Walmesley
Private Mullard
Private T. Harrison
Private F. Lamb
Private G. Clues
Private J. Jallimore
Private W. Boyd
Private C.L. Allen
Private J. Sturdy
Private J. Petrie
Private W. Beckwith
Private R. Yates
Private C. Mosley
Private J.C. Howes
Private H. Baillie
Private A. Rowlands
Private R. Hall
Private E. Higginbottom
Private H. Lawrenson
Private F.C. Mulvey
Private A.E. Pearce

Private A. COPPACH
Private T. GROOM
Private C.H. HOOPER
Private A. MARSH
Private J. TYSON

THE MERITORIOUS SERVICE MEDAL.

Regimental Quarter-Master-Sergeant A.J. FORD
Regimental Quarter-Master-Sergeant W. O'BRIEN
Company Quarter-Master-Sergeant A. JONES
Sergeant W.G. EDINGTON
Sergeant T. MUNCASTER
Sergeant GRAHAM
Sergeant CONOLLY
Sergeant H. KENNISTON
Lance-Corporal R. GRAYSON

FRENCH DECORATION. MEDAILLE MILITAIRE.

Company Sergeant-Major P. BYRNE

BELGIAN DECORATION. CROIX DE GUERRE.

Corporal H. READ

RUSSIAN DECORATION. CROSS OF SAINT GEORGE.

Sergeant H. CHISNALL

MENTIONED IN DESPATCHES.

Major-General F.W. RAMSAY, D.S.O.
Lieutenant-Colonel LORD H.C. SEYMOUR, D.S.O.
Lieutenant-Colonel F.W.M. DREW, D.S.O.
Lieutenant-Colonel H.K.S. WOODHOUSE, D.S.O.
Lieutenant-Colonel C.G. BRADLEY, D.S.O.
Major J.W.B. HUNT, M.C.
Major F.S. EVANS, D.S.O.
Major S.C. BALL, M.C.
Major J. MAHONY, D.S.O., R.A.M.C.
Major P.G.A. LEDERER, M.C.
Major N.L. WATTS
Major A.W. FULTON
Captain B.W. HOWROYD
Captain J.H. HALLIWELL
Captain D.H.D. WOODERSON, R.A.M.C.
Captain H.H. COVELL

Captain E.D.H. STOCKER
Captain W.R. PERRY
Captain R.C. WILDE, D.S.O., M.C.
Captain E. ASHTON
Captain C.B. JOHNSON, M.C.
Captain A.G. WARDE, M.C.
Second-Lieutenant C. NOTT
Regimental Sergeant-Major F.W. MILLER, M.C.
Regimental Quarter-Master-Sergeant A.J. FORD
Company Sergeant-Major J.C. WARD
Company Sergeant-Major J. OWENS, D.C.M.
Company Sergeant-Major R. GRAYSON
Company Sergeant-Major J.J. SNAITH
Company Quarter-Master-Sergeant A. JONES
Company Quarter-Master-Sergeant J. MEADOWS
Sergeant J.E. SMITH
Sergeant T. BALL, M.M.
Corporal R.L. ROBERTS
Lance-Corporal E. MOSS
Private W.J. HANNA
Private A. BOWYER